ONE JUMP AT A TIME

ONE JUMP AT A TIME

My Story

NATHAN CHEN
WITH ALICE PARK

Foreword by Vera Wang

18 17

HARPER

An Imprint of HarperCollins*Publishers*

HarperCollins books may be purchased for educational, business, or sales
promotional use. For information, please email the Special Markets Department
at SPsales@harpercollins.com.

An extension of this copyright page appears on page 224.

FIRST EDITION

Designed by Bonni Leon-Berman

Library of Congress Cataloging-in-Publication Data has been applied for.

ISBN 978-0-06-328052-6

22 23 24 25 26   LSC   10 9 8 7 6 5 4 3 2 1

For Ma, Da, Alice, Janice, Tony, and Colin:
Couldn't have done it without your unconditional
love, support, sacrifice, and guidance.

CONTENTS

Foreword by Vera Wang   ix

Prologue   1

1   How It Started   5

2   The Skating Life   33

3   "America's Hope"   65

4   Dread   77

5   New Challenges   109

6   Pandemic   129

7   Building Resilience   149

8   Taking a Different Approach   167

9   A Second Chance   189

Epilogue   217

Acknowledgments   221

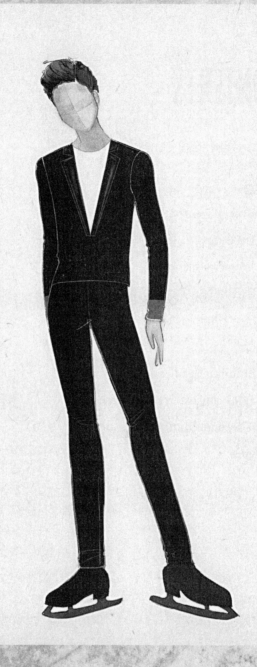

FOREWORD

What can one say about someone who, at such a young age, has achieved so much, and with such humility and grace? For me, as a Chinese American, and ironically, an ex–competitive figure skater myself, Nathan's journey seems all the more admirable, if not astounding!

As Americans, we have a long and storied history of World and Olympic figure skating champions; however, as is true with so many other disciplines, our sport had to evolve for so many reasons, and on so many different levels. Nathan brought that other level by helping to create an entirely new hypothesis for competitive skating with jumps we could never have dreamt of, and his own particular brand of effortless, almost casual style so unique and captivating in its nonchalance and originality. But this is not only a story about athletic achievement; it also represents a very personal tale about growing up in a large, boisterous, irrepressible family, with strong traditional Chinese values juxtaposed within a cultural norm of enormous freedoms, unlimited possibilities, and the relentless quest for change that so defines American culture. For these many reasons, Nathan's story is so unique.

Skating is a deceptive sport. The enormous toll it takes on both mind and body is incalculable, and the training and discipline it requires so imperceptible, that what often appears effortless actually defies physics. This is not a pastime for the faint of heart, nor is it an inexpensive pursuit.

And, as is so often the case, achieving anything, particularly Olympic gold, can be an extremely lonely pursuit and involves great sacrifice. Nathan's dream, I am certain, did not materialize all at once, but in Salt Lake City, where he was born and where the Olympics were held in 2002, so something about that Olympic magic must have intrigued him early on. In his case, his prodigious talent, passion, and drive all helped to create a future champion.

Our first meeting was at the Carlyle Hotel in New York City, on a cold, rainy winter day in 2017. It was just us; his mother, Hetty; and his agent, Yuki. I had by then dressed some of the most amazing Olympians and was fearful I could not come to the table yet again with the amount of thought, creativity, and innovation necessary to dress another celebrated champion. That responsibility can be daunting.

Nathan was also on the verge of exploding onto the global stage, and beginning to explore his own sense of style, intent on performing in something cooler, looser, hipper, very contrary to the body-conforming costumes so typical of competitive looks in the past. During lunch, as I was trying to coax him out a bit, I initiated a whole other line of conversation. "What do you want to do after skating?," something that might seem odd to ask a future champion in the making. I had seen so many incredible athletes ponder this eventuality, after devoting their entire youth to such a singular goal. So my very existential question was sort of my way of getting to know him. Without a second's hesitation, he said college, and in that moment I knew immediately who he was, and exactly how far reaching his ambitions lay. He had a plan B, and as it turned out, that became Yale. Yale got lucky, as did the world of figure skating!

To be perfectly transparent, I wasn't sure I could interpret Nathan's creative impulses, and he did push me out of my comfort zone, politely at first, but steadfastly, as time went on. One has but to see the very obvious evolution from our first costumes to those of the 2022 Olympic season. "I can't wear a one piece and perform that many quads." So it was really Nathan who educated me as to the amount of freedom he needed to perform at that level, while it was up to me to bring a creative edge to his technical concerns and ever evolving aesthetic. Interpreting a skater's program, choreography, and unique style is a complex exercise to begin with, but standing out at the Olympics can be even more challenging.

His courage in establishing his own boundaries not only in how he dressed but how he changed the sport technically and creatively represents a tale of singular determination mixed with equal parts humility, self-examination, and intelligence.

Ultimately, to be able to forge your own path, despite any odds, and to achieve at such an elite level without forgetting where you came from, or those who helped you along the way, that is what truly defines a champion. These are perhaps Nathan's truest accomplishments, and unlike most biographies, this is perhaps only the first chapter!

I am so proud to have played but a small part in this story but look forward to all I believe he will continue to contribute to the world. Nathan, thank you for bringing your own standards of excellence and magic to a sport we all love and adore. You have also laid a credible foundation for young people everywhere, while helping to support Asian Americans at such a significant moment in our history.

Vera Wang

Vera Wang and Nathan at the Figure Skating in Harlem 25th Anniversary Gala at Gotham Hall in April 2022.

ONE JUMP AT A TIME

PROLOGUE

My skating career has always been intimately tied to the Olympics. I took my very first, tentative steps on the ice at the practice rink for the 2002 Salt Lake City Winter Games—the same rink where figure skating legends like Michelle Kwan and Sarah Hughes practiced their programs before they had Olympic medals hung around their necks. The practice rink was located in the Salt Lake City Sports Complex, which the locals call Steiner, and every time I skated there, I couldn't help but feel the Olympic spirit. The rings were everywhere, and there were graphics of the Olympics, like a huge picture of speed skater Apolo Ohno, all around.

I can't remember ever not thinking that skating would bring me to the Olympics. Right from the start, I associated skating, and being an athlete, with the Games. I'm sure a lot of that had to do with the fact that when the Games were held in my hometown in February 2002, I was two years old; so growing up, it was impossible to avoid getting caught up in the excitement that the Olympics inspire.

My mom took a picture of me with my two brothers in front of the Olympic cauldron at Rice-Eccles Olympic Stadium, and you can see the Salt Lake 2002 motto, "Light the Fire Within," and the flags from the participating countries flapping in the breeze. Salt Lake City, especially then, was a very Olympic-driven town. Growing up there cemented in my mind the idea that being an athlete meant you went to the Olympics: to be a skater was to be an Olympic skater.

My mom is a big sports fan, so not long after I started skating, my family, like so many others, watched the 2004 Summer Olympics on television. It was the year Michael Phelps won six gold medals. Watching Michael's accomplishments in the pool, and especially the shiny hardware around his neck, must have made an impression on five-year-old me. The day after seeing one of his medal ceremonies, I decided to create my own version of the Games at the rink. At Steiner, there is a door that opens to let the Zamboni drive on and off the ice and looks toward a huge flag of the USA. My mom says I stood by this door and started singing the national anthem. When she asked me what I was doing, I told her I was pretending I had won a gold medal, so naturally I had to sing the anthem.

Fifteen years after I took my first tentative steps on that ice, I found myself at my first Olympic Games, competing for the gold medal in men's figure skating. It was a dream I had worked toward my entire life.

But my debut at the Olympics didn't quite go as I had imagined it. I was a nervous wreck. Minutes before I took the ice, I could hardly feel my legs. As I waited to be introduced, I was shaking and I barely heard my name as it was announced. Somehow I skated across the ice to take my position.

As I waited for my music to begin, I looked up and then I saw them. The Olympic rings. The rings I had seen every day skating at Steiner, the rings I had seen everywhere in Salt Lake City for years when I was a kid. The rings that had given me inspiration through countless hours of training and years of sacrifices.

I saw those rings and I froze.

What happened next was the most challenging experience I've lived through—but also the one from which I've learned and grown the most, both as an athlete and as a person. At my first appearance at the Olympics, I skated two of the most error-filled short programs I have ever performed, in front of millions of people on one of the world's biggest sports stage. Even as a toddler, I don't think I made that many mistakes in a single program. I went from thinking I had a real chance to win the gold medal, to seventeenth place after the short program, and ended up fifth overall. It was an emotionally draining and sobering experience.

Skating is a very methodical sport. You learn skills in a very logical progression—first you pick up basic stroking and how to generate power from bending your knees and pushing off the edges of your skate blades. Then you move on to your edges and learn how to adjust your body to skate on the inside and outside parts of your blades going both backward and forward, and then you pick up crossovers to build more speed. When you start jumps, you begin with a single revolution, and then add doubles, triples, and quads as you gain strength and refine your technique.

The competition levels are also laid out very methodically—from local and regional events to national competitions, and from pre-preliminary all the way to novice, junior, and finally the senior level. It's all iterative; and each new skill or level builds on the previous ones, so it's difficult to skip steps and leap over different levels.

That's a lesson that my mom, who has been an integral part of my skating career, always emphasized. No matter how much I struggled in practice, or how disappointed I was if I hadn't skated well in one particular competition, she reminded me that each of those challenges was only one step in a bigger journey. You have to take things one step at a time and construct a strong foundation before adding on new skills. That layer-by-layer strategy helped me join a generation of athletes that set a new standard in men's figure skating, to become the first athlete to land five different types of quads in competition. It's the same strategy that both got me to my first Olympic experience and helped me to move on from the disappointing results.

That approach drove me to a second chance at the Olympics and another opportunity to tell a different story and script a different outcome. But I knew I had many more steps to take before I could make my Olympic dream unfold the way I had always envisioned it would.

This is the story of how I finally got there.

1 HOW IT STARTED

千里之行始于足下

**A journey of a thousand miles
begins with a single step.**

When I was three years old, I took my first steps on the ice. I must have liked it enough for my mom to enroll me in a Learn to Skate program at Steiner. Steiner is a huge facility dedicated to all kinds of sports and includes swimming pools, a weight room, and two sheets of ice—one that is Olympic size and one that is NHL regulation size. My older sisters had skated there, after learning to skate at a different rink in Salt Lake City before these were built, my brothers played hockey there, and it was only a couple miles away from our house, so it was only natural that my mom took me to Steiner—first to watch my brothers and sisters skate and then to get on the ice myself.

I'm the youngest of five. My oldest sister, Alice, is ten years older than me; then there's Janice, Tony, and Colin, who is three years older. Once they started school, I ended up spending a lot of time with my mom. I was pretty lonely without them, so she worked really hard to find things to do to fill up the days. Sometimes we went to the library to check out books; and sometimes, after one of her friends suggested it, we even went to Costco so I could run up and down the big aisles and check out the food samples.

At the time, my dad was at the University of Utah in Salt Lake City getting his PhD in pharmaceutics and pharmaceutical chemistry. For a while we lived in a small student housing apartment. It was pretty crowded for our big family of seven, so my sisters shared one room, while my parents and the boys shared the other room, with my brothers in a bunk bed and me in my crib.

My mom was busy with five kids running around, so my older sisters helped with a lot of babysitting duties when I was a toddler. Soon after I was born, we moved into a house, but it needed a lot of work, so my older siblings pitched in to paint and clean before we could move in. I was too young to do anything but lie around in a carrier and watch them work.

My parents always made education and learning a priority for us. They made sure that all of us had the opportunity to learn not just from school, but also from whatever activities interested us. Those values were passed down from their own parents during their childhoods in China, where education is seen as the gateway to everything—the first step toward whatever kind of success in whatever field you chose. All of us were accepted into the Salt Lake City school district's extended learning program (ELP) for gifted students beginning in kindergarten through junior high, and then my siblings went on to join the International Baccalaureate program at West High School in Salt Lake City. My brothers and sisters now look back on everything we were able to do—skating, chess, dance, violin, viola, cello, piano, hockey, and gymnastics—and we're really amazed at how my parents managed it. With five kids, that wasn't always easy, and financially things were often tough.

My mom in particular didn't want us to miss any opportunities to learn. Her father had often told her that success was like an equation of talent multiplied by hard work multiplied by opportunity. Talent is the factor we're born with, hard work is the factor we can control, and opportunity is the factor we need to recognize and hold on to. You can't really change talent that much, but you can change hard work and opportunity. And because it's a multiplication equation, if any one of the factors were zero, then the result would be zero.

My mom never forgot this formula and lived this philosophy in raising us. The result was that our days were packed, but each of us was able to learn so many new skills that we continue to enjoy and benefit from today.

My parents have both had interesting journeys to the United States. My dad was born in southern China in Guangxi Province, bordering Vietnam and close to the South China Sea. As with so much of that part of the country, Guangxi is known for its natural beauty, especially its caves, rivers, and unique mountain formations of limestone, gypsum, and dolomite. These are soluble rocks, which means water erodes them, creating spectacular caves with the amazing stalactites and stalagmites that the area is famous for. When Colin graduated from high school in 2014, my dad took him to see his hometown and visit Guilin and tour the beautiful Li River. I hope I get the chance to see them one day as well.

My dad was raised by a single mom. Before he was born, my grandfather and grandmother divorced, so my dad lived with my grandmother. I don't think my dad ever saw his father. He even took my grandmother's last name, Chen.

With her encouragement, my dad was very focused on getting the best education he could. He earned his medical degree from Guangxi Medical University, one of China's oldest medical institutions. After graduating, he headed northeast to Beijing to pursue a master's in military medicine at the Academy of Military Medical Sciences. The professor he worked with had research labs in both Beijing and at the institute's satellite campus in Tianjin, which was an hour and a half drive southeast. From time to time, he would work there.

My mom was born in Beijing but later moved with her family to Tianjin. My mom's father worked as a professor and research scientist at the Academy of Military Medical Sciences's Tianjin campus. That's where my parents met.

My maternal grandfather got his medical degree from Mukden Medical College in Shenyang in the northeastern part of China. He hadn't started out thinking he would be a doctor. His family had a small clothing business, and made fur gloves and hats. My great-grandmother wanted to expand the enterprise, so she sent my grandfather to Japan to earn a business degree. He didn't talk about his time there much, so our family isn't sure whether he was in Osaka or in Tokyo, but while he was there, the second war between China and Japan broke out. Fortunately, my grandfather was able to return home. After seeing so much suffering and illness upon his return, he decided to go to medical school to learn how to heal people.

My mom's mom also was a doctor, and earned her medical degree in Shanghai; and my grandparents met while they were both working at a hospital there. My grandmother was a general physician, and my mom remembers her taking care of patients with all kinds of ailments, and even doing small surgeries if needed.

When my mom was in junior high school, she had the choice of learning English or Japanese as a second language; and her father, who spoke Japanese fluently after his time in Japan, urged her to pick Japanese. He had been really impressed with his experience in Japan and thought learning Japanese would help my mom get a postgraduate education there.

In addition to being academically focused, my parents were also pretty athletic, so I definitely owe my love of sports to them. My dad competed in high jump in college, and says that though he was often the shortest athlete, he often got the most cheers from the crowd. My mom became a pretty good swimmer. But her dad thought swimming wasn't going to lead to a stable career: he saw it only as a fun way for her to get some physical activity. My mom was interested in fashion design, and after graduating from college, began teaching textile manufacturing in Tianjin. At her father's suggestion, she applied to be one of fifty teachers that China was sending to Japan in a special program to earn advanced degrees in education. She applied, passed the difficult exam, and was accepted, and thought about spending a year in Japan.

By this time, though, she and my dad were married, and my dad had gotten accepted at Southern Illinois University, Carbondale, to pursue more postgraduate work. He was thinking about moving to America with my mom to continue his studies. Even though she didn't speak English, my mom thought there would be more opportunities to study and grow in the United States, since Japan was more restrictive about student visas.

Still, my mom didn't want to disappoint her dad, so she applied her typical logic to the situation. Since she would need to attend a three-month training program before going to Japan, she told her parents that she would apply for a visa to the United States while she attended the training. If the U.S. government granted the visa, she would join my dad in America. If not, she would go to Japan.

Her visa came through very quickly, so the decision was made. My dad came to the United States in January 1988 and my mom followed in December.

Things were not easy for them. My mom had to give up her dream of studying fashion design; and as a student, my dad wasn't earning much. As our family grew, finances became really tight. They couldn't even afford English lessons for my mom, so she decided to learn it on her own.

Before my sisters went to school, my parents would speak to them in Chinese; there are videos of them when they were really young speaking Chinese. But as soon as they started preschool, they stopped, and started using English. Because Alice and Janice spoke English to each other, my mom started picking it up. She said it wasn't too hard, because young kids use simple words and she learned along with them by watching educational children's shows on TV. My mom encouraged all of us to speak English because it was the best way for her to learn.

When my older brother Tony was about four or five, she enrolled everyone in Chinese classes at the local Chinese church on Saturday mornings, so we wouldn't lose our ability to speak the language. However, after Tony started playing in chess tournaments, which were held on Saturdays, the same time as the Chinese classes, they ended up missing a lot of classes, since the whole family would follow him to tournaments in Utah as well as surrounding states. Alice and Janice also started to play, so my mom figured Chinese classes could wait. All of us can still understand a little spoken Chinese, because our parents speak Chinese to each other and use a mix of Chinese and English with us. When Janice was eleven and Tony was eight, my parents sent them to China for a summer chess camp with the Chinese national chess team in Beijing, so they could improve both their chess and Chinese skills and learn more about Chinese culture. In just a few days, they were able to communicate with their training mates and coaches at the camp.

My mom also picked up that we wanted to be as much like all the other kids as possible, and that included sounding like them. When my sisters started using English at home, my mom sensed that they didn't want to be different from their classmates. That's the constant struggle with children growing up in immigrant families—finding the right balance between assimilating and not losing the identity or values that come from your unique cultural heritage. Alice admits to now feeling that maybe she suppressed her Chinese culture and embraced and adopted American values a little too quickly back then, which set the precedent for the rest of us to do the same.

But I think that if we had to do it over, we'd choose the same path. My parents supported our choices—they really didn't want us to feel different, and thought that in order to help us succeed, we needed to do what we could to fit in.

As the youngest, I don't remember as much as my siblings do about those early years, but my sisters recall my parents having fights over money. Still, my parents made it a priority to ensure that we could pursue whatever activities interested us. With Tony traveling all around the country to compete in chess tournaments, my parents wanted to make sure he could continue competing, since he was obviously talented, especially for his age. My parents had to search for ways to financially support our interests. Being a part of the University of Utah helped out a lot. Since my dad was an alumnus there, we could take advantage of all kinds of programs and scholarships that let me and my brothers and sisters take music and dance lessons. Alice, Janice, and I took modern dance classes at Children's Dance Theater, which was part of the university; and Colin took engineering and chemistry classes at the university's after-school and summer programs. After getting his PhD, my dad worked as a research scientist and the first employee in a biotech start-up, Salus Therapeutics. It was created in 1999 by his graduate adviser, professor Duane Ruffner, based on their novel antisense library technology that was demonstrated by my dad's PhD research on anti-HIV antisense and ribozyme molecules. Four years later, Salus was sold to another pharmaceutical company to become its research and development division. But within a year, that parent company had to lay off nearly all its employees, including my dad, when a couple of their drug candidates didn't get approved by the Food and Drug Administration.

Those were really hard times for our family, but because I was so young, I didn't know how difficult things were. There was a period of a few months when I was in elementary school when I didn't have any skating lessons and only worked with my mom because we couldn't afford them.

Throughout my career, but especially in those early years, I could not have continued skating if it hadn't been for the generosity of sponsors and anonymous donors. In the summer of 2007, my dad read about the Michael Weiss Foundation, which supports young skaters with scholarships, and he sent them an email about my fledgling skating progress. Michael was a phenomenal U.S. figure skater in the late 1990s who competed in two Olympics and won two World medals. While he was still competing, he created the foundation to help up-and-coming skaters financially. To my dad's surprise, Michael wrote back, saying the foundation accepted applications only at a specific time, but that based on what my dad had told him I was a "special young man." Soon afterward, he sent my dad $200 in an express mail envelope to help with my skating expenses.

That was just the start. Over the next ten years, I received $75,000 in scholarships from his foundation. This money was crucial to keeping me skating. Michael's generosity was so important to my career. He sets such a great example of what it means to give back to the sport. His foundation has helped so many others, including top competitors like Adam Rippon, Ashley Wagner, and Mirai Nagasu, all of whom became national champions.

I was also fortunate enough to have the support of so many generous people, beginning with coaches, who never charged me their standard fees and spent countless extra, unpaid hours on the ice with me, to skate and blade makers, including Harlick, WIFA, Jackson Ultima, and John Wilson, all of whom have donated their products to me, and to my many skate sharpeners who at a moment's notice were ready to help get my blades ready, pro bono.

To help pay for my skating, my mom learned medical terminology from my dad's Chinese-English medical dictionary, took interpreter training classes and exams, and became an interpreter for local hospitals, helping Chinese-speaking patients communicate with their doctors. But the work wasn't always steady; she went whenever they called. She also took on a variety of different part-time jobs while I was in school to continue supporting the family. She even cleaned houses for a while, after a friend suggested it as a way to earn some extra money.

I'm only now starting to really appreciate the sacrifices my mom in particular made for me. Skating is an expensive sport, and she never made me feel that my lessons were becoming too much of a burden financially. One way or another, my mom always found a way to help keep me on the ice.

As the "little brother," I was always in a rush to copy and follow what my brothers and sisters were doing. And that probably made me a little more active and fearless than they had been. My sisters and I took piano lessons, so we had an upright piano in our house that doubled, occasionally, as a teaching tool for my mom. When we did something wrong or dangerous, she would sometimes place us on top of the piano and tell us why we couldn't run or scream or touch things that we shouldn't. When you're really little, that height from the top of the piano is no joke. My mom knew it wasn't high enough for us to accidentally get hurt and would stand by just in case but thought that our being so high would imprint on our brains that whatever we had done was wrong, and to never do it again.

When I misbehaved and it became my turn to perch on top of that piano, I just jumped off. My mom was so surprised. She couldn't believe how easily my little body could handle such a big leap. I laughed and made it clear that I wanted to be put back up on the piano to jump off again. She didn't know what to do. She certainly couldn't plop me back up there, because obviously it wasn't having the disciplinary effect she was going for.

That piano got a lot of use from my sisters and me. Somehow my brothers never picked it up; Colin played the cello and Tony ended up playing drums and trumpet in high school. Watching my sisters play, I must have wanted to do the same. When I was one and a half, my parents took all of us to Toys R Us and told us we could pick out whichever toy we wanted for a Christmas present. I apparently grabbed a set of sports balls, which included mini versions of a soccer ball, basketball, and football, and a tiny toy piano. I was so transfixed by the piano that I stayed in that aisle for a long time. My mom tried to convince me to follow my brothers and sisters to look at other things, but I planted myself in front of that piano and refused to budge. Once we had it back home, I spent hours playing it, but I'm sure I just generated a lot of random noise.

Following my siblings to Steiner to skate became one more activity to fill the day. I was still a toddler the first few times I got on the ice, so I didn't do much—I mostly stood around, trying to get used to the foreign feeling of the slippery ice underneath my feet. But I clearly liked it, because when the public sessions ended and everyone had to leave the ice, I stubbornly stayed put. When the ice monitor came to gently guide me off so the Zamboni could do its job, I started bawling because I didn't want to leave. I'm sure my tantrum was embarrassing for my mom. But it was me just trying to stay on the ice for as long as I could.

Maybe it's because I got on the ice at such a young age, but I've always loved skating. I thrived on the feeling of power that came from zipping silently across a pristine, freshly cut sheet of ice. I wanted to play hockey, like my brothers did, but since I was three and so tiny, my mom was worried that the curved blades on hockey skates would make me fall backward. She ordered a pair of figure skates for me online instead. There are pictures of me in those skates—and, yes, they're white, so a lot of people assumed they were hand-me-downs from my older sisters. The white skates were cheaper than the black skates, and my mom didn't know anything about the sport back then, so she thought, what difference does the color make? She was right, and those skates were the gateway to a career that would bring me the greatest joy and fulfillment, as well as some of the deepest frustration and heartache. Skating has shaped who I am today and taught me about how to create success from failure and fulfillment from disappointment. I'm still in the process of learning those lessons, but skating created the foundation for my development. My parents still have those first white skates somewhere, and I'm glad they do.

After sending my brothers and sisters to school, my mom would bring me to the public skating sessions, which started at nine in the morning. Since most kids were in school at that time, the rink was generally pretty quiet. But skating around in circles got boring pretty quickly, so my mom thought that being in a group lesson might make things more interesting. She signed me up for my classes in the Learn to Skate USA program in September 2002. That first level was called Snowplow Sam (the first thing skaters learn is how to stop, by pushing your skate blades out in the shape of a "V," like a snow-plow.) Whatever I learned in the group class, my mom would help me to practice at the public sessions.

That's how my mom's involvement in my skating career really started. From the beginning, she was 100 percent committed to my skating. She felt strongly that if I took lessons once or twice a week, the rest of the week I should practice what I'd learned. If I didn't practice and improve, then I would end up wasting time going over the same things at my next lesson. Especially since money was so tight for our family, she wanted to make sure all her kids got the most out of whatever lessons we took.

My mom instilled in me the drive to keep pushing and working on something until I mastered it. Because of her, I learned how to be disciplined and push through the hardest times in my career, no matter how tough things got. She didn't hang out in the snack bar or relax while I was on the ice; she sat rink side at every lesson and paid attention to every detail of what I was doing, whether it was in a Learn to Skate class or working with a coach in a private lesson. She brought me to the rink every day to skate at the public session and practice what I had learned. She thought that was just what parents were supposed to do when their kids took any kind of lessons, whether it was in sports or music or anything else.

But it didn't feel like work, because my mom also made it really fun. When I learned new elements, she would reward me with red Swedish gummy fish, my favorite treat at the time.

All that practice paid off, and I picked up the skills quickly. My teacher at the time, Stephanee Grosscup, saw the progress I was making in the group classes and suggested to my mom that I start taking private lessons once a week. Stephanee became my first coach, and made me fall in love with skating. She taught me the basics: how to glide, how to push off from an edge, and the sheer joy that comes from pressing into the ice with your skate blades and propelling yourself around the rink faster and faster and faster. She laid a great foundation for me. There's a picture of me with Stephanee from my first competition where I'm wearing a blue vest and a red bow tie and those white skates. My program was just basic elements like a snow-plow stop, skating a couple of steps, and a bunny hop. But still, I won!

I couldn't get enough of being on the ice. A few years after I started figure skating, I also started playing ice hockey, following my older brothers. My mom thought it was a good idea, because it's a team sport and I would be with other kids my age. Plus, she thought that playing hockey would build strength and power in my legs. To do well, I would also have to learn strategy and make quick decisions to execute plays. But my mom's initial hesitation about hockey skates proved prophetic. The first few times I stepped on the ice after putting them on, I of course slipped and fell backward. My mom found this hilarious and to this day still laughs at the memory. After falling three times, just to make her stop laughing, I finally got my balance on those blades. For a few years, I went back and forth between the two rinks at Steiner for figure skating and hockey, and I loved it—and got really good at quickly changing from figure skates to hockey skates.

I picked up new skating skills pretty quickly because I tend to be good at copying what I see others do, but it also helped that I was pretty fearless. If Stephanee asked me to try something new, I wouldn't think about it long enough to get scared or worry about not being able to do it—I would just try it. I'd fall the first time, but I would try again and fall again and try again. That would get me really mad, and I remember crying a lot on the ice. But I would keep trying, even though I was upset. I remember at times when the other skaters fell, or couldn't get a new element, they would cry and stop trying. Their coach would get frustrated, point to me, and jokingly say, "Look at Nathan, he's crying but at least he's still skating!"

It also helped that my mom dangled just the right incentives for me. When we saw other skaters doing a doughnut spin—a spin that starts with your leg behind you and ends with you curving your back and bending your leg parallel to the ice to grab your skate blade with the opposite hand from behind, turning your upper body and leg into a doughnut—she said, "That's cool, let's try it! If you get it on the first try, I'll buy you a doughnut." At the next public session, I tried it and nailed it the first time, so she had to make good on her promise.

To help me develop a competitive streak on the ice and to find a fun way for me to do repetitions of the same element, she would play a game called superheroes vs. villains. She would start by naming her right hand the superhero's name, and her left hand the villain's name. Each time I performed something correctly, she would put a right-hand finger down and that would be a point for the hero. When I made a mistake, a left-hand finger would come down and that would be a point for the villain. The goal was to get the superhero's fingers all the way down to zero before the villain's fingers did. I would get so mad if all the villain's fingers came down first, and so she told me the only way the superhero could win is if the hero won the next two rounds of "battle." Without thinking, I immediately went forward to play another two rounds with her and quickly did up to twenty-seven repetitions. She would always be playing these games with me on the ice so I wouldn't get bored with either skating around in circles or mindlessly practicing the same things over and over again.

With so many older brothers and sisters, my competitive streak only developed further—everyone else was older, and could do things better than I could, but that didn't stop me from trying to beat them. It got to the point where Colin didn't want to play games with me when we were kids because I always wanted to win and would throw a tantrum if I couldn't.

A few years after I started skating, I competed at my second Utah Winter Games, a festival that included events in speed skating, figure skating, and hockey. I skated a program to "Three Blind Mice," and my mom made my costume: a one-piece gray outfit, a black vest, and a red bow tie. I was one of only two skaters, and I finished second, but I received a distinguished skater award. When I got back home, my brothers asked me how I did, so I said, "I finished second."

Tony said, "No, you got last." That made me so angry, and I started crying and screaming that it wasn't true.

I appealed to my mom and asked if Tony was right and she said, "You can say you finished second, or you finished last, it's just the same." That didn't really help, and Tony's comment continued to annoy me, fueling my competitive drive (he says he doesn't remember it at all, but does admit it sounds like something he might have said).

My sisters weren't as harsh. They actually sparked my early interest in dance and music. Alice was obsessed with ballet, and by default so was Janice. When I was young, they gave me dance lessons and created dance routines for me to perform that nobody ever watched. I was always pretty easygoing when it didn't come to competing, and never complained, unlike my brothers, who wouldn't put up with anything my sisters wanted them to do.

My sisters joke that their crowning achievement came before I started skating, during the 2002 Winter Olympics in Salt Lake City. Technically, they beat me to the Olympics because that year they participated in the opening and closing ceremonies as Children of Light. And the story of their audition again shows the great lengths my parents went to so that their kids could take advantage of opportunities like that. The night before the audition, Tony, Alice, Janice, and Colin had a chess tournament in Las Vegas, Nevada, so our entire family drove all night in order to get back to Salt Lake City in time for Alice and Janice to try out. They made it, of course. But in typical Chen fashion, after the audition, we immediately drove back to Las Vegas to continue the multiday chess tournament.

The Children of Light symbolized the motto of those Games, "Light the Fire Within," because the idea was that a child who was caught in a snowstorm was able to find his way using his lantern and his own inner strength to overcome his fears. He passed on this "fire" to hundreds of other kids, and my sisters were among them. Their costume was a furry white coat, white hat, scarf, and gloves; and they carried a lantern. Of course they had to dress me up in their gear and send me out onto the ice during one of the public sessions. I must have looked like a little yeti, but thankfully I don't remember that at all.

With my mom's encouragement, I continued to skate, and began winning trophies and medals at local events. At these competitions, I proudly wore the costumes that my mom sewed. She learned most of her skills by volunteering at the Children's Dance Theater, where my sisters and I took dance classes, and spent hours and hours sewing my costumes until I was around twelve.

After a few years, the coaching staff at Steiner started to change. A new coach from a different skating club had arrived and started working with some of the younger skaters and tried to convince my mom to switch from Stephanee. But my mom wasn't sure what to do. Stephanee was a really good teacher and understood how to connect with young children. When she taught me the scratch spin, she told me to pull my arms in front of me close to my body as if I were squishing a giant marshmallow. She made things easy for a four- and five-year-old to understand.

But as I started progressing, my mom was tempted to change. She felt that on the one hand, no matter how good your kindergarten teacher was, at some point you have to move on to first grade. Because I was starting to pick up more skills, including jumps, my mom thought I needed a new coach who was more focused on jump technique. But she wasn't convinced that the new coach at Steiner was right for me.

My mom started to ask some of the skating parents about coaching options, did her research, made a lot of calls, and found someone who she thought was a better fit for me: Karel Kovar. I was sad to stop working with Stephanee, but we never lost touch and she remains a part of my skating career. Even after we no longer lived in Salt Lake City, my mom would sometimes call her for advice when we were struggling with making important decisions or didn't know what to do next in my skating career.

Karel didn't live in Salt Lake City, but about an hour's drive away in Ogden, so my mom drove me there twice a week. I still wasn't even in grade school yet, so that worked out well. Karel was from Czechoslovakia and had skated pairs with his sister. He also trained with Alexei Mishin, the famous coach in Russia who coached many Olympic champion individual skaters and pair skaters, so my mom trusted his technical expertise.

Karel really set up my jump technique. He taught me the mechanics of how to jump each of the six different jumps—the toe loop (often shortened as toe), the Salchow, the loop, the flip, the Lutz, and the Axel. Some jumps—the toe, flip, and Lutz—start from a toe pick that vaults you into the air, known as toe jumps. With the others—the Axel, Salchow, and loop—you create a deep edge with your blade to propel yourself into the air without the help of the pick, known as edge jumps. Karel introduced me to a unique rotation position, teaching me to pull my arms across my torso like a seatbelt. To help make this second nature, he put me in a vest fitted with sensors where my hands should touch and when I achieved the correct rotation position the vest would make a beeping sound. To this day, I continue to use this rotation position (but thankfully without the help of the beeps). He worked with me on all my double jumps, from double toe, the easiest, all the way to the double Axel, the hardest. The Axel continued to be one of the most challenging jumps for me, even when I started doing triples and quads.

Karel also introduced me to another former skater with great jumping technique, Jozef Sabovčik, who skated for Czechoslovakia. Jozef was the Olympic bronze medalist in 1984 and known as "Jumpin' Joe" for his amazing jumps. He and Karel were good friends and he was living in Bountiful, Utah, with his family. While he mostly toured, I took some lessons from him when he was available. Jozef was the first coach who told me not to stop in the middle of a program if I made a mistake while I was in a run-through.

Karel was very strict but kind. He gave me a new perspective on skating and helped me start training more seriously.

But jumps weren't the only thing that make a strong skater and my mom knew this, so I also took some lessons from an ice dance coach at Steiner, Kent Weigle. He worked with me on improving my edges and basic skating skills. And it didn't stop there. My mom also thought I could benefit from dance and gymnastics classes to build up the coordination and strength I needed for jumps. Because figure skating is all about rotating on a vertical axis, whether for spins or jumps, she thought that it would be good to balance skating with gymnastics, which includes rotating on a horizontal axis. After I turned seven, she found a gym in Bountiful where a Russian couple coached and signed me up for classes in the summer of 2006. She drove me to Bountiful for gymnastics in the morning, then back to the rink in Salt Lake City for skating in the afternoon. I liked gymnastics a lot, and did well enough that the coach invited me to join the boys' team, which competed at state- and regional-level meets. But the team trained six days a week and there was no way I could maintain both gymnastics and skating once school started. My mom didn't want me to drop gymnastics, and decided to move me back to the recreational class once a week, which upset my gymnastics coach. She told my mom I had good coordination and that cutting back on my classes would ruin my gymnastics career. But she wasn't aware of how serious I was about skating at that point, since I had never mentioned it. Once she understood that, she made an exception for me and let me stay on the team and train with them one day a week, on Fridays, and go with the team to meets. I'm grateful that she did, and in March 2008, I won the all-around at the Utah Boys' State Gymnastics Championships in St. George, Utah.

I ran into the same dilemma with ballet classes. I started taking lessons at Ballet West, a major dance company in Salt Lake City that also had a dance academy, because my mom thought it would improve my artistry and musicality on the ice. Just as with skating and gymnastics, anyone who was serious about ballet took classes nearly every day, which I couldn't do. My mom spoke with the director, Peter Christie, who allowed me to dance three days a week. I ended up dancing the parts of the nephew or Fritz in Ballet West's *Nutcracker* every year, and danced in their productions of *Swan Lake* and *Sleeping Beauty*, while I was in elementary school.

My days were getting packed with activities. After a full day of school, my mom would pick me up and bring me to Steiner, where I would practice for two hour-long freestyle sessions, then some days I would have hockey there. Other days we would get back in the car and she would take me to ballet class; and on Friday we drove to gymnastics. Once I got home, I had dinner, did some homework, practiced the piano, and went to bed, then repeated the whole thing every week.

During this time, I never questioned why I was skating, and never questioned why my mom was devoting so much time to me and my skating lessons. In my family, that level of commitment was just a given. My mom didn't discriminate when it came to keeping on top of what her kids were doing. Alice was a member of the drill team at school and had practices at 6 a.m., so my mom would wake up at 5 a.m. to get her ready. After a full day at the rink with me, and after making dinner for everyone, she would stay up until one or two in the morning to help us kids work through whatever homework problems we had, and then would get up early to drive Alice to drill practice the next morning. She would sit and listen as Alice, Janice, and Colin practiced piano, violin, viola, or cello and help them if they didn't get certain notes right. My dad spent more time with Tony, supporting his chess; they would drive several hundred miles to St. George in southern Utah to take chess lessons from a Russian grandmaster on weekends, and Tony won many national and state scholastic chess championships. Because of him, everyone also played; and Janice became Utah's women's chess champion twice. This started before I was born and continued even when I was a baby; my mom would watch my brothers' and sisters' games holding me in her arms. It was normal for the Chen children to devote a lot of time to our activities. For me it was skating. I was so young when I started that I wasn't really aware of how different my life was because I spent so much time at the rink; it was where I wanted to be. I happily did what my mom told me to do—joining the Learn to Skate classes or taking lessons with my coaches. It never occurred to me that most other kids didn't spend as much time at the rink as I did.

So, naturally my mom was serious about helping me to improve my skating. She would set a goal for me of doing, say, ten clean double flip jumps at a practice session. If I didn't finish all ten by the end of the available sessions, she would pack me and my skates in the car and drive to another nearby rink to finish up the jumps. I also had trouble with my double Salchow jump for a while, which I would under rotate, meaning I'd finish the last quarter or half turn of the jump not in the air but after landing on the ice. Fridays, I would practice the jump at my skating session, then we'd drive thirty minutes to gymnastics in Bountiful. After gymnastics, my mom would drive me to another rink in Bountiful so I could squeeze in even more practice on the double Salchow. Her philosophy was that practice makes perfect, and the more I practiced, the cleaner my landings would be. We spent so much time at the rink that people joked we should just bring our sleeping bags there and move in.

She was always very positive about training. If I couldn't land jumps, she would always say, "We'll call this day a falling day," and urge me to keep trying the jumps, even if I continued falling and would get frustrated. A lot of coaches and parents would let their children stop trying and pick it up again the next day. But she wouldn't let me quit. "If today was a falling day," she would say, "tomorrow will be a landing day."

At one session, when I kept falling on a jump, another mom who was watching must have taken pity on me and asked my mom why she didn't stop me. "Aren't you afraid he's going to learn the habit of falling?" she asked. My mom wasn't worried at all. Falling was part of learning, and with enough learning, she knew I would get it.

In the year that I started kindergarten, my mom and I didn't have time to drive out to Ogden to see Karel, so he was kind enough to come a few times a week to Salt Lake to give me lessons, which continued for about three years. Eventually, my mom felt that having a coach always at the rink would be more beneficial. In the summer of 2007, when I was eight, there was a coach at Steiner who held a summer camp for his skaters, and my mom was a little jealous of how he prepared his skaters and how well they trained. She can't remember if she went to the coach first, or if the coach approached her after seeing the progress I was making, but he offered to not only teach me but also find a sponsor who could support my lessons. My mom really wanted a coach who could see me practice every day, so she decided to leave Karel and let me start to work with the new coach.

But somehow the new coach found out that I was also taking gymnastics classes after school, and he questioned the need for a sponsor to pay for my lessons if my parents could afford gymnastics. My mom told him the classes were only a few dollars an hour and that gymnastics was acting as off-ice training for me to build strength for my skating. She explained that our finances were barely covering all the activities my siblings and I were doing, and that adding in daily lessons would be financially impossible for our family. But the coach wasn't convinced, and I never ended up working with him.

I was stranded. But, as usual, I never knew, because my mom stepped in to find a solution. She didn't want me to stop doing what I loved because of financial reasons, so she was determined to find someone who would coach me. And for about the three months until she did, she stepped in and structured every one of my daily skating sessions—guiding me on how many jumps to practice and trying to help me get more consistent with landing them. That got her in trouble with the rink management and some of the other skaters' moms. They would comment in her hearing that I no longer had a coach because no one wanted to train me. That really hurt her feelings, and she remembers it as one of the most difficult times she experienced in my skating career.

It really bothered her, but it also motivated her. She was determined that nothing would hinder my skating progress. She went back to researching available coaches. She remembered hearing about a good jumping coach, Akop Manoukian, who used to coach in Salt Lake City. Akop was a men's singles skater from Armenia who was known for introducing more acrobatics to the ice (fun fact—Akop was Will Ferrell's stunt double in the movie *Blades of Glory*). My mom decided to reach out to him to see if he had time to work with me, but unfortunately he had moved to Jackson Hole, Wyoming. He still had a home in Bountiful, however, and said he would give me lessons whenever he was there.

My few lessons with Akop were really productive, but my mom still needed a more permanent coach for me, and consulted a board at the rink that listed all the skating coaches and their bios. She immediately noticed a young Russian coach, Genia Chernyshova. When my mom told me she had set up a lesson for me with Genia, I was a little afraid at first. I had seen her at the rink with her students and she seemed extremely strict and serious. Still, my mom convinced me to give her a try, saying we would start with just a fifteen-minute lesson once a week.

I didn't know that my mom could afford only fifteen minutes of Genia's time. Around this time, my dad had decided to start his own company, and as a result, our family's finances grew even tighter. So when my mom approached Genia for lessons, she asked for fifteen-minute lessons per week and promised Genia she would help me practice the rest of the time. As with so many coaches throughout my career, Genia was very generous and agreed. From the start, Genia rarely stuck to that limited lesson time. The fifteen minutes grew to thirty, then an hour, and eventually she trained me for two sessions a day, six days a week—and never asked my mom for additional fees.

Genia could still be a little scary, and when she learned I was taking gymnastics, she was worried about my getting injured. She told me she would be really upset if she ever saw me limping into the rink. She also worked at the Utah Olympic Oval, where the U.S. speed skating team would practice, and sometimes she would take her students there to skate at the ice rink at the Olympic Oval. I guess the coach of the speed skating team noticed me zooming around the ice and asked Genia about whether I would be interested in picking up the sport. My mom heard her tell the coach loudly that I was a figure skater, and her student, so I was off-limits. Then she told me that if she ever saw me in speed skates she would come after me!

Genia really made it possible for me to start competing and moving up through the levels established by U.S. Figure Skating. In order to attend out-of-town competitions, especially the smaller ones at the starts of their careers, skaters and their families normally have to cover their coaches' airfare, rental cars, meals, and hotel accommodations, not to mention the daily training fees and their lost coaching income while they are away from the rink—and these costs really add up. Other than airfare, Genia never asked my mom to pay for anything, and she would even stay with us in our hotel room to keep our costs as low as possible. She also knew my mom couldn't afford to buy the stuffed animals that people throw on the ice after skaters compete, so if the competitions were in Utah she would ask her husband to come and throw them onto the ice for me so I wouldn't feel left out.

In 2008, when I was nine years old, I qualified to compete at the Junior National Championships in Lake Placid, New York, my first at the intermediate level. Genia knew that the cost of her flight alone would be too much for my family to handle, but she still wanted me to experience competing at the Junior National Championships. So, Genia told my mom that she and her husband had decided to "vacation" in Lake Placid that year. Since she would be there anyway, she could help put me on the ice and my mom wouldn't need to pay for any of her expenses. Knowing this clearly was a cover, my mom was very grateful, and off we went. Lake Placid, like Salt Lake City, is very steeped in Olympic tradition. The 1980 Games were held there, including the memorable Miracle on Ice U.S. hockey victory over the Soviet Union. To get to the competition, we had a long drive up into the Adirondack Mountains, past small resort towns and beautiful lakes. We passed the old ski jumping training site on the way into the town, which isn't really a town but a main street with a few hotels, stores, restaurants, and several rinks. The most prominent feature in town is the outdoor speed skating oval, where Eric Heiden became the first skater to win gold in all five distances in that sport.

Before the trip, Genia promised me I could skate on the Oval if I did well. I finished second, but unfortunately the Oval was closed for the season. I didn't mind, because I remember playing in the snow and having a great time.

Both my mom and I learned so much from Genia that proved invaluable as I got older and moved up the ranks. Like Karel, Genia had also been a pairs skater in Russia, and she had a meticulous training system that I still miss to this day. Genia was a master at mapping out how much training I needed, and dialing that level of intensity up or down depending on how close I was to a competition, or whether I was injured. Every day, she had a new plan for me, and told me what warm-up exercises I needed to do, how long I should warm up, and how many run-throughs of each program I would do. Everything was super clear, and that's exactly what I needed at that stage in my career.

Unlike with Karel, I trained with Genia every day. She was very strict about how precise things had to be—every arm movement, every head position, and every stroke I took on the ice she meticulously laid out for me. She pushed me very hard physically, too. Building on the foundation that Stephanee and Karel had started, Genia developed me into the skater that I am today. Without Genia's knowledge, I wouldn't know how to train and prepare a program for competition. She provided me with the first steps toward understanding how many sets of a program I needed to do during training to develop consistency and how to challenge and push myself so that I could overcome anything that might give me trouble during competition.

Genia was so good at guiding me through training that I was still able to win my first novice championship in 2010, even though I had injured my knee and couldn't jump at all until days before the competition. At the time, I was also dancing in the *Nutcracker* and had a New Year's Eve matinee performance. Right after the performance, I went to skate at Steiner. My knee hurt a little but it didn't bother me enough to stop skating. But, during a program run-through, I fell on my triple toe, which caused my knee to start hurting more. The next day, Genia saw it and thought it was serious enough for me to take a couple of days off to recover. It was still painful after resting, so she brought me to a doctor at the Olympic Oval. The doctor said it wasn't a big deal but that I needed to give it time to heal and that I absolutely could not jump for at least a week and a half. Genia masterfully planned my next few weeks on the ice, guiding me to skate run-throughs of my programs without jumps and certain spins that might aggravate the injury. To make me feel more tired as if I had expended the energy to jump, she added weights to my ankles. Even if I wasn't at 100 percent physically, we trained hard every day doing only the things that didn't cause me pain. The timeline was challenging though, because once I was healthy enough to start practicing my jumps again, I would only have a few days of training before competing at the novice National Championships. Genia was concerned that it wasn't enough time to make my jumps consistent enough to compete and she suggested to my mom that I withdraw from the competition, but my mom disagreed. Even if I finished last, my mom thought it would be a good experience to compete at the novice level for the first time.

Three days before leaving for the championships, we started training my first jumps, beginning with single jumps. The next day, we did doubles; and the day before I left, we trained my first triple in two weeks. On the day that I was leaving for Nationals, we ran my first full program with triples. I ended up falling on two of my jumps in the long program at Nationals, but I skated a strong short program and won my first novice title.

At the time, I didn't feel like I deserved to win since I had made two big mistakes in my long program, but I was reminded that figure skating isn't just about how you perform in one program, but how you perform in both. Each program is equally valuable, and I learned the importance of making the most out of every chance I had to skate. I was so excited to hear that I'd been invited to skate at the exhibition on NBC with all the other champions from the different disciplines. My mom and I decided that since I had this extra opportunity to perform, I should re-skate my long program with the elements that I missed and try to perfect them this time around. I landed everything during this skate, and afterward I had my first interview on national TV, with Andrea Joyce. That's when she asked me in which Olympics I was hoping to compete. Many years prior, I had asked my mom when I would be able to compete in the Olympics, and she told me that I would be old enough to compete in 2018. So with the quiet confidence of a ten-year-old Nathan, I said, "2018."

2 THE SKATING LIFE

不积小流无以成江海

It is impossible to form a river and sea without accumulating small streams.

Shortly after I got back from the novice National Championships, the 2010 Olympic Winter Games started in Vancouver, Canada. On the night of the men's individual free program, I was eating dinner at home with my eyes glued to my TV. Evan Lysacek was competing in the 2010 Olympic men's individual free program. I held my breath as he nailed jump after jump. After the competition was over and the final scores came up, the highly sought-after number 1 appeared next to Evan's name. The camera panned back to Evan and his coach, Frank Carroll, hugging each other with joy as they realized he had just become an Olympic champion.

I always knew I wanted to be an Olympian, and seeing Evan win his title only solidified my desire to experience that moment myself.

Getting to those 2018 Olympics, however, was going to take a lot more learning, and far more fortitude than I could have imagined at that age.

I continued to pick up new skating skills quickly and I really liked the challenge of learning new elements. I loved watching other skaters, especially the top athletes I saw competing at big events on TV, and I tried to emulate what they were doing. I would pretend that I was one of the Olympic skaters whom I had seen on television.

During the public skating sessions, when there weren't too many other skaters there, I would pretend I was 1984 Olympic gold medalist Scott Hamilton, or 1988 Olympic gold medalist Brian Boitano, or even 2002 Olympic bronze medalist Timothy Goebel. I couldn't copy their jumps, of course, but that didn't stop me from pretending that I could. I learned how to do Scott Hamilton's excitingly fast "Hamilton turns." I tried to rotate my jumps 'Tano style, with one hand above my head as I rotated, made famous by Brian Boitano. I dreamed of one day landing the quads that Timothy Goebel so easily landed. Timothy was the first skater to land a quadruple Salchow in competition, and the first to successfully land three quads in a single program—the original Quad King.

As I continued working toward my dream of the Olympics, the sport began taking me to places I never could have imagined. When I was six, Karel invited me to perform in my first out-of-town ice show, a Christmas show in Las Vegas. He played Santa, and after I finished my program, he carried me around the rink on his shoulders in a group number. I gradually started skating in more shows, traveling around the world and gaining experiences that helped me learn to appreciate the pure joy of performing in front of people.

After the 2010 novice National Championships, I had the chance to travel to China for the first time and skate in a show in Hangzhou, thanks to my godfather, David Liu. David is a talented skater who competed at three Olympic Games for Taiwan, and watched me compete at the 2010 Nationals. He told my parents that I reminded him of himself when he started on the ice, and he asked to be my godfather. It was the first time I was a member of a cast of professional skaters, and it was a great learning experience to watch how they interpreted music and entertained audiences. David introduced me to Richard Dwyer, who skated with the Ice Follies and is known as "Mr. Debonair," the holder of the Guinness World Record for the longest professional skating career. David choreographed a fun piece to "Singing in the Rain" that I skated with Richard, as the youngest and oldest members of the cast—I was ten and Richard was seventy-five.

While I was in China, I also met one of the kindest people I will ever meet, Ted Wilson, the manager of the World Ice Arena in Hangzhou. Ted had retired from performing with the Ice Capades and devoted himself to promoting figure skating in parts of the world where it wasn't as accessible, such as China, Hong Kong, and the United Arab Emirates. He was active in the Ice Sports Industry (ISI), an organization that promotes recreational figure skating by building and developing ice rinks, and founded ISI Asia in 2000. Ted passed away in October of 2013 and his legacy will forever live on in the countless athletes who now have access to ice rinks around the world. I will forever be grateful to Ted for his support of my skating and inspired by his tireless efforts to spread the sport he loved so much to all corners of the world.

Those trips to China were also especially meaningful to me personally, since I got the chance to meet many of my relatives for the first time. My mom brought me to my grandma's house, and they showed me around China. My mom and I walked up and down the Great Wall, and my mom was eager to show me other historic sites around Beijing. But instead, I told her I only wanted to see the Beijing Zoo. She couldn't understand why, since I could go to the zoo in the United States, but she indulged me, and I got to see all the animals, including the famous pandas. I was reminded of my childhood fascination with that zoo when I was back in China for the 2022 Winter Olympics, since the bus always drove by the Beijing Zoo on the way to the rink.

Winning the novice title also opened a lot of doors for me back home. I was invited to perform in the summer ice shows in Sun Valley, Idaho, for the first time in 2010, and have been invited to perform there every year since. The show is a highlight of the off-season for many skaters, and we perform in the year-round outdoor rink at the resort there. I love skating in that show because I can often bring my family. It was also a good place to try out my new skating programs—as well as other tricks. I learned how to do a backflip there from Ashley Clark, a professional skater in the show, and performed my first one on that outdoor rink.

I continued the slow climb through the different levels—from juvenile into intermediate, then novice, juniors, and finally seniors. While the Olympics were always in the back of my mind as a long-term goal, during those years there was always a more immediate task of the next competition or the next level to reach.

In juvenile, I was not very successful. A lot of the other skaters at that level were doing double Axels, but I couldn't land one yet. I remember my mom had me watch a video of Jason Brown, who had an excellent double Axel, so I could learn from his technique. While I was in novice I got my triple Salchow and triple toe. But there were other skaters who were landing far more advanced jumps. Genia knew that since I didn't have all the technical elements yet, I needed to quickly develop the rest of my triples and to maximize points in other departments. She helped me to focus more on my artistry, or as much as a ten-year-old can have. One of Genia's fortes was concentrating on the little details, from how I held my fingers to where I looked during each part of the choreography to how I interpreted each phrase of the music. She homed in on those skills and made sure my skating became more polished and that every element was executed as cleanly as possible.

My training with Genia was intense but fruitful. I remember before I got my triple toe, she had me jump double toes for an entire training session. This went on for days, and my mom started to get irritated, wondering why I was doing so many repetitions of a jump

I had already mastered. After a few more days of this, Genia told me to try a triple toe and just like that, on the first few tries, I landed my first triple toe! Under her watch, I started landing my triple toe, then triple Salchow, then triple Lutz, and finally triple flip, and started working on the triple loop.

Landing those jumps made me confident that I was on the right track. Once I learned those triple jumps, I worked on putting them together in triple-triple combinations. A lot of the other skaters at the novice level, who were working on the same combinations, were a little older than me. While I wasn't entirely successful with all the triple-triple combinations, I never stopped trying to land them consistently because I believed that if I could land the jumps the older kids were doing, I would have a bit of a head start. But landing triple-triples wasn't the end goal, and I still had a long way to go.

Around that time, on the junior circuit—the next level up, which was a few years off for me—at the international level, I saw guys doing triple Axels and quadruple jumps, things I hadn't even considered trying. I knew that if I wanted to compete against these skaters, I would have to progress even more quickly and keep adding revolutions.

My mom realized this, too, of course, and started thinking about how I could continue to progress with my jumps. Before I started with Genia, I had started working with Akop on learning the double Axel and triple toe.

One day, my mom asked Akop's opinion for how I could continue developing my technique. He told my mom, "If you think I'm helpful, there's a guy I know who would be even more helpful. He's way, way, way better than I am in teaching jumps."

My mom and I were immediately interested. He told us the coach's name was Rafael Arutunian and, like Akop, he was Armenian. Rafael had coached in Russia before moving to the United States, and had worked with a lot of really great skaters—Michelle Kwan, who had won two Olympic medals and multiple World titles; Sasha Cohen, who won silver at the 2006 Turin Olympics; Jeffrey Buttle, the Canadian men's bronze medalist at those same Games and the 2008 world champion; and Mao Asada, the 2010 Olympic silver medalist and a three-time world champion from Japan. Akop offered to contact Rafael to see if he would consider teaching me.

At first, Rafael was hesitant. He was already busy with many competitive athletes skating at the international level, and he was only interested in putting in the time to develop a younger skater if he knew the skater was fully dedicated to the sport. He was only eighteen when he started coaching, and early in his career he had worked with junior skaters who quickly moved up the ranks. By the time Akop told him about me, Rafael had already been coaching for more than three decades and was focusing on more established skaters. Fortunately, Akop was insistent, and told Rafael he should really reconsider because he thought I was talented for my age and was really serious about skating. Rafael finally agreed, and my mom and I drove the ten hours from Salt Lake City to the Ice Castle International Training Center in Lake Arrowhead, California, to meet him.

It was magic at first sight.

It was a perfect pairing. Akop was right; Rafael, or "Raf," as I came to know him by, is the best jump technician I've ever met. When we first connected, in 2010, I was desperate to have a consistent triple-triple combination and triple loop. I asked him to help me since I was constantly falling so hard every time I tried them.

We started with the triple toe–triple toe and within a few lessons I started landing my attempts. Raf is a master at breaking down each part of a jump, perfecting those parts, and then putting them back together. He understands the smallest details of how a jump works and can provide direction on how to generate the most power and torque to execute each jump perfectly. When I first went to work with him, he joked about how silly he thought my training approach was. He asked me: If there was a giant brick wall in front of me, would it be better to try to punch through the wall, or, would it better to take a step back and look for a way to walk around it? Since I was little, my mom and I spent countless hours watching videos of the best figure skaters land their jumps. However, we didn't know the minute details that were necessary to land them myself. I would resort to performing attempt after attempt to slowly learn what I needed to do.

That's just how I had learned new elements up to that point. As a kid, that repetition was necessary to build muscle memory, but as you start moving on from triple-triples to triple Axels and quads, that repetition quickly becomes too punishing on your body. Raf started to teach me how to break down a jump, from body positioning, to directions on the ice, to timing and rhythm. Slowly, I started to understand how to walk around that brick wall.

Raf was impressed with the fact that I, thanks mainly to my mom, was so serious about learning what he had to teach. Just as she had done throughout my time in Utah, my mom sat near us when Raf coached me and wrote down everything he said so we could work on the exercises he gave me when we went back to Salt Lake City. When we returned to Lake Arrowhead after several weeks, he was satisfied to see that I had put all his advice into practice, dutifully executing what he had asked me to do. That level of commitment really convinced him to continue working with me.

But the distance was a problem. For about a year, throughout 2011, my mom and I would make the long drive to Lake Arrowhead about once a month. We had a Prius, and it was a lifesaver in those years—we ultimately put more than two hundred thousand miles on that trusty car. Because I was still in school, we would go whenever we could, especially over holidays or long weekends. We'd leave on Friday evening after family dinner and drive back late Sunday night so I could get as many hours at the rink as possible before we had to leave. My mom usually found cheap hotel rooms for us, down the mountain from Lake Arrowhead, which meant I had to spend an hour on the road before and after my training with Raf each day. After he found out about that, Raf let us stay in his basement guest room whenever it wasn't occupied—just one of the many, many kindnesses he extended to us over the years.

Those drives seemed endless, and we would often stop at a gas station in southern Utah to sleep for a few hours and then continue driving the next morning. But at least I could sleep or catch up on my schoolwork in the car. I know it was hard on my mom, but she never complained. She said she liked driving at night, since there was less traffic, but it must have been really tedious.

The more time we spent at Lake Arrowhead, the more we both felt that the training environment there was better for me than the one in Utah, so the effort was worth it. During that time in Lake Arrowhead, Raf was coaching alongside the legendary coach Frank Carroll who was the coach of Evan Lysacek, and who had also coached Michelle Kwan, a Chinese American role model and icon and someone whom I had watched on TV. Denis Ten, of Kazakhstan, who would go on to win bronze in 2014 at the Sochi Olympics, and Tatsuki Machida from Japan, who would win silver at the 2014 World Championships, also skated there. Training with top-level skaters who were doing more challenging jumps than the skaters back home gave me the exposure to quads and triple Axels I needed to trust that I could do the same as well.

After a year of driving back and forth, I really pushed my parents to make the big decision that my mom and I would move to California to train with Raf, while the rest of my family stayed in Salt

Lake City. By that time, the only children at home were Colin, who was a sophomore in high school, and me. Alice was away at college at Emory University, Janice was attending Johns Hopkins University, and Tony was at University of Southern California. My mom wanted to wait until Colin graduated from high school before moving for my skating. But after getting a taste of what it was like to train with world champion and Olympic-level skaters, I told my mom I really wanted to train there every day, not just a few days a month.

I knew it would be hard to leave Genia; she had truly helped me so much over my first years as a skater and was the reason I was ready to start working with Raf.

But while she pushed me very hard, I knew I needed to make quicker progress technically. My sights were always set on being able to do a triple Axel and quad jumps, and it seemed like I was so far away from that target. How was I going to take the next step if I hadn't even mastered the triple-triple or the triple loop?

In 2012, just before Nationals in January, when I was twelve, my mom and I moved to Lake Arrowhead, while my dad and Colin stayed in Salt Lake City.

For me, the move was life-changing. The rink at Lake Arrowhead is truly one of a kind. It's located high in the San Bernardino Mountains, an hour and a half drive northeast from Los Angeles, in a very rustic, woody setting. The rink is custom-made for figure skating. Unlike other rinks, where people also play hockey, Ice Castle doesn't have barriers, so three sides of the ice run flush with the floor sort of like an infinity pool, while another side has a huge mirror. So many legends trained there, not just from the United States but international skaters like Chen Lu from China and Surya Bonaly from France. Shen Xue and Zhao Hongbo, who were the first Chinese pair skaters to win Olympic gold in 2010, also skated at Ice Castle.

I always sensed that great skating legacy while I trained there, and really enjoyed the idea of skating on the same ice as past notable athletes. Anthony Liu, the owner, kindly let us stay at the camp house that was part of Ice Castle's summer training camp housing, free of charge, until we could find a place to live. My mom later found a small cabin close to the rink. It was so deep in the woods that the only way to get there was via a dirt road that was unpassable in the winter when it got snowy and icy. Most of the winter, we parked in a nearby church parking lot and walked home through the woods in deep snow.

In addition to a new skating facility, I also had to find a new school so I could continue my education. In Salt Lake City, I was enrolled in the extended learning program (ELP) which, in practice, placed all their students one grade ahead. So, when I enrolled in the California school district, while my age placed me in seventh grade, because of ELP, I was placed in the eighth grade. I was placed in the ninth grade for math, however, and so I had to split my time between Mary Putnam Henck Intermediate School for my core classes and Rim of the World High School (from which Michelle Kwan graduated) for math. Because there were so many elite skaters that had gone to school there in the past, the administrators were flexible about allowing me to take all my electives through independent study.

After skating, my mom would take me to the Lake Arrowhead Resort and Spa to work out at the gym. We didn't have Internet in our cabin, so after my workout I would complete my homework in the resort's lobby until midnight or so.

And just because I was in a different city didn't mean my busy schedule eased up. I was also keeping up with gymnastics and ballet. I continued ballet classes with Michelle Mills, who taught at Lake Arrowhead, and my mom eventually found a gymnastics club in San Bernardino for me to take classes. I even continued to play hockey for a while and joined the local team, the California Wave. My mom really honed her driving skills chauffeuring me to all those practices up and down the mountain from Lake Arrowhead.

Soon after we moved, I competed for the first time at the junior level at Nationals, in January 2012. Genia was still officially my coach for that competition, although I went there with Raf (Stephanee came as well to help support me). He drove my mom and me to the event in San Jose. Genia had choreographed a free program to *The Godfather* soundtrack, which I picked out. I remember that we had to skate a footwork sequence that stretched across the whole rink, and half of the sequence had to be completed on one foot only. At the time, I was so small, so covering that much distance with quick and intricate direction changes made my legs burn. Still, Genia's choreography helped me win my first National Junior title.

After Nationals, my serious skating training began with Raf. He coached me through two more years in juniors. I was traveling to more competitions, including ones overseas, and skating was becoming even more of a priority in my life and my family's. The skating season starts in the fall with competitions through October, November, and December, until U.S. National Championships in January and World Championships in March. That meant my family couldn't get together for Thanksgiving and Christmas, since I wasn't able to take any time off from training. My siblings and I got used to that, and we tried to see one another whenever we could, sometimes at my competitions.

I was constantly amazed at how quickly Raf could see mistakes and correct my elements. I'm a skater who works entirely on instinct and feel when it comes to things like jumps—I can feel if my takeoff isn't right, or if my body isn't in the correct place to execute a good jump, for example. Raf could also sense this and would immediately pick up on whatever I was doing wrong. He gave me corrections on things I knew felt wrong, but couldn't actually figure out how to adjust. He is the best at providing jumping exercises that trained my body as much as my mind, so that when it came time to perform, my body would know exactly what to do.

He also had me work every day with his assistant Nadia Kanaeva on other skills to improve the quality of my skating. She helped me to continue building my fundamentals, things like body position and edge control, which are critical for good jump technique; and Raf knew that without them, I wouldn't be able to master quad jumps. Raf and Nadia planned every aspect of my competition programs, with the ultimate goal of preparing me for the Olympics. One of Raf's strategies to create more strength for my jumps was borrowed from gymnastics. On tumbling runs, gymnasts increase the power and height of their jumps by stringing together several flips. He asked me to pack multiple jumps into a very short time frame to increase momentum in the same way. This became somewhat of a signature for my programs while I competed in junior, as I started to get accustomed to stacking multiple jumps in the second half of my program, which meant I earned bonus points for them since skaters receive an extra 10 percent for doing jumps in the latter half of a program.

I enjoyed Lake Arrowhead, but my time there didn't last long. Less than two years after we arrived, the owner of Ice Castle decided to close the rink. Everyone had to move, and we followed Raf, who switched to coach at East West Ice Palace in Artesia, which was owned by Michelle Kwan and her family.

Our move to East West marked a shift in how I felt about skating. Maybe I was homesick or just getting older and more aware of the challenges in pursuing this goal of getting to the Olympics. It wasn't as easy as just dreaming anymore. It took all of my energy and time and even that wasn't always enough. My frustration with my skating started growing.

After the initial excitement of working with Raf on learning new jumps, I had hit a wall. I had spent months working on my triple Axel, but it was still really inconsistent, and I didn't have any inklings of a quad yet. I was thinking about moving from competing at the junior level to the senior level, and aspiring to make the top three at senior Nationals. My goal had always been about being competitive at a World and Olympic level. I knew I was in no position to compete against the top men in the U.S., and if I couldn't even make it to the top of senior Nationals, I had no shot on the world stage. And if I couldn't compete internationally, all this sacrifice would be for nothing.

I started to doubt if all my hard work would ever pay off. It didn't help that I was recovering from a bunch of injuries that were affecting my training and slowing my progress.

On top of all of that, I missed having a group of school friends and being a regular student. When we moved to Irvine, I had to switch to remote learning because the public schools there weren't as flexible, and I couldn't take classes for only half a day and skate in the afternoons. Plus, the ice time at East West was mostly in the morning, from six to two, so I ended up skating in the morning, doing my office and playing hockey or doing gymnastics in the afternoon, and taking classes online from Connections Academy in the evening. I was feeling so frustrated with everything that I asked my mom if I should quit and just go to high school in Irvine like a regular student.

My mom reminded me that if I stopped skating, we would have to go back to Salt Lake City. Skating in competitions was what got me a little funding to support my lessons and ice time, through U.S. Figure Skating. I was also starting to compete internationally, representing Team USA. Depending on where I placed, I received some prize money to support my training. If I didn't skate, we couldn't afford to continue paying rent to stay in California.

I really liked Irvine; and as I thought about it more, I realized that quitting wasn't an option. Yes, things were getting harder, but everything I had already put into skating would be wasted if I quit. And in another year, I would be moving up from the junior ranks to finally compete at the senior level. It was another big step and I had always been looking forward to it.

I decided to continue.

A large part of what was feeding my unhappiness with skating back then was not only my slow speed of progress but also my inconsistent record in the junior ranks, which were the result of a lot of escalating injuries. During those early years, I had Osgood-Schlatter in my knees, which is common in teens. Osgood-Schlatter is an inflammation of the area where the tendon below the kneecap attaches to the shinbone. During growth spurts, the bones, muscles, and tendons keep changing, which can put strain on the places where they attach. Add to that a high level of physical activity like jumping and the exertion can really cause problems—and a lot of pain. During long car rides, for example, my knees would get so stiff and painful that I would have to massage them and warm them up for a few minutes before I could even get out of the car. There weren't many conventional medicinal options available to me other than ice my knees and take over-the-counter painkillers if they really hurt. I ended up trying a new treatment called prolotherapy to help expedite the healing. Prolotherapy is a complementary medicine approach that involves injecting a sugar solution into the joint to promote growth of connective tissue, which can lessen pain. It helped a little, but the good thing is that Osgood-Schlatter goes away once you're done growing and your growth plates close.

I also had low back pain every now and then, and a shoulder growth plate injury that prevented me from pulling my body into a tight rotation for a jump. The biggest problem, though, involved my hip. I started experiencing spasms of pain and eventually needed surgery.

As a result of all my injuries, my record at the junior level was pretty hit-or-miss; I was either pretty good at competitions or performed quite poorly. There was never a middle level where I was able to maintain a consistent level of training and competence. When I was thirteen, I became eligible to compete in the junior Grand Prix series for the first time. My first event was in Linz, Austria. I'll never forget the day I received my Team USA jacket; I was so happy I wore it to the rink and Raf was really proud to see me in it. I won my first junior Grand Prix event, and landed two triple Axels, setting a new scoring record.

But not long after that, my left ankle became so painful that I couldn't bend deeply into the outside edge of my triple Lutz. At my next Grand Prix event in October 2012 in Croatia, after I competed the short program where I landed a triple Lutz–triple toe combo, I couldn't twist my left ankle and was in a lot of pain. My mom never traveled with me to international events, so Raf and the medical team made the decision that I would withdraw from the competition. My foot hurt, but after a few hours of rest I felt I could have competed with all my jumps besides the Lutz, so I was upset. I called my mom, frustrated because I didn't want to withdraw. I really wanted to finish the event because if I didn't, I couldn't accumulate enough points to place top six in the series to qualify for the Junior Grand Prix Final. But the medical team thought it was best that I not continue skating, so I had to follow their advice.

In a little over a month, I was scheduled to compete at the Pacific Coast Sectionals. I decided to stay off the ice for the entire month in order to recover, but wasn't sure if that would be enough time to heal completely. I spoke with Mitch Moyer, the senior director of athlete high performance for U.S. Figure Skating, about withdrawing since

I wasn't sure if I'd be able to be at 100 percent by Sectionals. He told me that if I didn't compete at Sectionals, I wouldn't be able to compete at Nationals, so I decided I had to go ahead. For the next month, my mom drove me to Eastvale, down the mountain from Lake Arrowhead, every day to do strength training and swimming to maintain my stamina. I wasn't able to start skating again until five days before the competition, but the off-ice training helped, and despite being away from the rink for so long, I came in second and qualified to compete at Nationals again.

I really wanted to compete at Nationals to defend my title, so I continued to battle through my injures. My left ankle was still really aggravated so I couldn't attempt any Lutzes, the jump that requires me to deeply invert my ankle. Once I got to Nationals in Omaha, Nebraska, the U.S. Figure Skating team doctor prescribed a new painkiller, but it gave me a headache and made me dizzy, so I had to stop taking it. The next day I felt better, but that night, I woke up really nauseous, and vomited and had diarrhea and a fever. It turned out I had a norovirus infection. Anything I drank or ate—including Gatorade, which the doctors recommended, and a tiny bite of bread—made me vomit. I was knocked out in bed. Everyone suggested that I withdraw, but I was already there so I insisted on competing. Somehow, I managed to skate through my short program. Since I couldn't eat or drink anything, before the free program, the medical team met and decided to give me a glucose and saline IV infusion in the arena before I went on the ice. That got me through that program, and while I couldn't defend my National junior title, I came in third. That was probably the toughest competition of my entire skating career in terms of how bad I felt physically. But I thought that if I could compete under such difficult conditions, then I could skate under almost any challenging circumstances in the future.

My final year as a junior, I did win the title back, which qualified me for the World Junior championships in Bulgaria. In the month between U.S. Championships and junior Worlds, Raf was in Sochi for the 2014 Olympics with Ashley Wagner, and I was back in California training by myself. One day, while I was practicing the triple Axel, I fell and used my right fist to brace myself. I ended up breaking a metacarpal bone in my hand, and my mom rushed me to urgent care. They splinted it, but they didn't put my hand in a cast to stabilize it, so I could see that the bone was still bent in an abnormal way. My mom thought I needed a cast, and drove me all the way to Salt Lake City to the Intermountain Primary Children's Hospital for another opinion. She always felt better when I got treated for my injuries in Salt Lake City, since we knew the doctors there. They ended up putting a cast on my hand. Having the cast on made me a little more comfortable with getting back on the ice to train, so I even practiced my jumps, holding my right hand close to my chest. Since Raf was at the Olympics, we didn't want to bother him about my hand. When he came back, he was surprised and upset that I had hurt myself and couldn't train properly for the upcoming World Junior Championships in Bulgaria, which he thought I had a good chance of winning. Regardless, Raf and I went, cast and all. My mom found some flesh-colored fabric to cover the cast so it wouldn't stand out so much, and I went on to win bronze. Afterward, Raf did tell me that he was very proud of me for fighting through the competition with a broken hand.

My relationship with Raf has been a well-rounded journey, and it has grown and evolved in the many years I have known him. I was so young when we first started working together, and many of the athletes he previously worked with were much older, so I might have expected guidance in a different form than he believed in giving. His coaching style was very different from Genia's or Karel's. From what I understood, Raf rarely took on students as a full-time coach;

he more often mentored skaters as a specialist for those who needed extra work on specific techniques. The ones he did coach exclusively were experienced competitors with many years of international competition under their belts, which I didn't have. Beyond an excellent jump technician, I felt I needed someone who would tell me exactly how many sessions I needed to skate, or how many jumps I needed to train in every session, or how many program run-throughs I needed to complete every day—just as Genia had.

Still, I learned a lot from Raf—he strengthened each one of my triple jumps and helped me improve the consistency of my triple-triple combinations. Before I ever attempted my first quadruple jump, he was already setting the foundation for me to land them, because from the first few times he watched me skate, he felt I had the ability to master them. All the exercises he asked me to do were geared toward the ultimate goal of learning quad jumps, long before I was even ready for them. But I didn't always agree with this plan; so at times, I started to feel frustrated because I believed it was more important to train the programs I needed to compete, instead of spending all of our time focusing on jump exercises.

Raf's training philosophy was so different from what I had been used to. As a kid, I liked to take the shorter route to accomplish my goals. Back then, if I didn't have someone constantly on my ass, pushing me every single day, I would not have learned to add on those extra repetitions in training. Karel did that for me, Genia did that for me, and certainly my mom did that for me. From the first day I started skating, my mom generally played a role of head coach. She had that Mamba mentality—if I gave 150 percent every day, I was going to realize my dreams.

With Raf, it was very different. He would say to me: To create a delicious dish, a chef needs to patiently select and precisely prepare each individual ingredient. Once the mise en place is complete, the dish will naturally come together. That's the philosophy he took in coaching me. He didn't think it was his job to command me around the rink, or tell me how to train each day, or force me to put my elements together, but instead believed it was his responsibility to take the time to prepare one ingredient at a time, in this case teaching me individual elements, so when the timing was right all of the elements would fall into place within a program. He wasn't going to lay out my daily training schedule as Genia had once. If I was in a lesson with him, we would work on individual elements, or jump sets, but if I wasn't in a lesson with him, he wanted me to take ownership of figuring out how many run-throughs of my programs to do, which parts I needed to practice more, and which elements I needed to practice on repeat so I could land them in competition. At the time, the one area of my competition preparation that he asked me to pay more attention to was the second half of my program. Generally, the latter half is harder for me to skate well, because I'm more tired and my legs are getting pretty spent by then. So, executing all my skills well takes a little extra attention, energy, and precision, which is what Raf emphasized. But in my inexperienced view, I felt that by focusing on only one half of the program, we were neglecting the similarly important first half. I knew he was right in asking me to strengthen the second half, but I couldn't figure out how to arrange my training so that I would have enough time and energy to work on all the things he expected me to do, as well as all the things I thought I needed to work on.

I couldn't figure out that balance on my own, and as a shy adolescent, I didn't have the courage to communicate with him in a way that an athlete should. I was too afraid to ask him to provide that guidance for me, or to even think I could ask for it. Both my mom and I missed Genia's style of training, and we felt lost without someone guiding my daily practice sessions. So my mom ended up taking on the role of structuring my day-to-day training plan, while

Raf concentrated on my jump technique and mapping out my jump layouts. Because Genia had set a good foundation, my mom tried to remember as much as she could about how Genia arranged her training sessions and re-create them for me in California. Early on, she joked to Raf that she was ready to retire from being my coach and hoped he could find someone else to oversee my training. As my mom, she didn't feel she was the right person anymore to supervise my practices. But Raf told her that she shouldn't stop.

Raf has a very particular way of communicating, which was very different from my previous coaches, and most people in general. His directions came in the form of fables, stories I had to read between the lines to figure out what he was trying to say. When my mom asked him whether I should be practicing on Sundays, for example, or take Sundays off, he said something like "Fish need to be in water; you can't take fish out of the water and give them a break and then put them back." I think we were supposed to understand from that that I should be practicing seven days a week.

When I was in my early teens, though, I was having trouble reading between those lines. I just wanted someone to tell me what to do and when to do it. While he was trying to focus on his own role and get me to take responsibility for my training, I interpreted his hands-off approach as indifference. When I was struggling the most, I felt that I had the least amount of help and support from Raf. And when I was doing really well, I had the most amount of support, which I found confusing. I remember once when I was struggling with my jumps—I would do a couple of them and either fall or pop them. I did this a few times at practice and Raf would turn his back on me. And I don't mean that as a figure of speech—he would physically turn his back and leave the rink. I didn't need anyone to give me hugs and kisses if I was making mistakes. But if I fell, I expected to receive some adjustments to make for the next attempt.

To be fair, when things weren't going well, I would ignore Raf in frustration, and sometimes skate away from him because I was feeling upset. Later, Raf explained that if he had inserted himself into those moments, I wouldn't have learned how to manage my emotions and make the corrections on my own, that I needed to in order to grow as an athlete. He knew his adjustments wouldn't be of any use until I was ready to listen and execute them. He always had reasons for what he did, but I didn't always understand what they were. For him, timing was always key.

Looking back, these growing pains were necessary in our relationship, and not that different from the ones any parent and child experience. Raf has always treated me like another son. And despite my desire for more of his guidance when I was younger, I knew he cared a lot for me. I remember that he had an expensive bike that he lent me on the weekends so I wouldn't be bored when I wasn't skating. I was too short to reach the pedals even after he lowered the seat, so he took out a saw and cut off part of the metal tube that held the seat to lower it even more. He even drove me all the way down the San Bernardino mountains to a mall one Christmas when he saw my shoes were getting worn and bought me a new pair.

More importantly, Raf, like Genia, was very generous with the time he spent coaching me. For most of the time he was my coach, we paid him very little, and certainly not his usual rate. Several times, he even gave back the money my mom had paid him. I don't think we ever really knew what his rate was, because he never asked for it and we just paid him what we could. He truly wanted to work with me to help me reach the potential he saw from the first day I arrived at Lake Arrowhead. When I was injured and had so little time to train for Pacific Coast Sectionals after my recovery in 2012, in my second year at the junior level, Raf told me that he would pay me a grand if I performed two clean programs. These were watered-down programs that he knew I could handle, so I figured he was just trying to help me financially, and also that he was proud of me for trying so hard to qualify for Nationals. I delivered, and he was very happy to make good on his promise.

Working with Raf, I was finally starting to land my triple Axel, and my first quad jumps—the quad toe and the quad Salchow. I landed my first triple Axel in 2012, just a few days before my thirteenth birthday. When I was fifteen, I landed my first quad—the quad toe. In addition to all the jump exercises, I had been working separately on my triple toe for a while to get more lift out of them so I could add another revolution. The first time I had tried a quad a few years earlier, when I was thirteen and training at Lake Arrowhead, it didn't go well. I couldn't really feel the rotations and control them, so I would fall and go sliding across the ice from all the force I generated. And because there are no boards at Lake Arrowhead like they have at most rinks, I slid right off the ice and onto the rubber-coated off-ice surface. On one of those falls, I hit my hip, hard. It was painful and scary—I was usually fearless, but I didn't want to practice the jump again for a while.

I knew I had to figure out what it would take to rotate myself around four times in the air and land safely, but it took almost two years until I felt ready to try again. This time, I went into my attempts with a little more understanding of the mechanics of the jump, thanks to Raf.

Going from doubles to triples is tricky, but doable. Triples to quads is an exponentially bigger step, both in terms of energy and the mechanics involved: in order to fit in a fourth rotation, you need to generate more torque and control the timing. And in order to do that, you need to create as much power as possible before the takeoff. You have to set up the direction of the jump just right, generate rotation at just the right time, and think about where you put every part of your body—your arms, head, your legs, your takeoff foot—to maximize rotation, jump height, and flow.

I didn't have all that down perfectly when I started working on the quad toe again. But I was starting to understand what it took and to visualize myself landing the quad toe. After a few days of training the quad, I got closer to finishing the rotation. One session, I tried about six or seven times, falling on some of them, popping out of others, but finally landed two of them. It was a huge accomplishment. Landing the quad meant I was that much closer to competing with the top-level skaters in the United States and internationally.

Inspired by that success, a few days later, I tried the quad Salchow and managed to land it. With this jump, as with my other quads, I didn't rely on the harness that some skaters use. It's a pulley some rinks have where you strap yourself in, kind of like you do before you go bungee jumping, and your coach will yank you up in the air while you spin so you can get the feel of the jump in the air without worrying about falling. I used it when I was a kid to learn triples and worked a bit on triple Axels and quads in a harness; but I always thought it felt too different from doing the jump unharnessed, so I preferred not to use it for quad training.

With the quad toe and quad Salchow, I was beginning to feel that I had the technical goods to compete at the senior level, and that I was ready for it since I had already been at juniors for three years. But, I hadn't qualified for senior international competitions yet and so I competed at the senior level at U.S. Nationals, while I continued to compete internationally at the junior level.

That year, Raf's assistant, Nadia, choreographed both my short program, to Michael Jackson, and my free program, which was set to a Chopin concerto.

At the 2015 National Championships in Greensboro, North Carolina, I planned to include two quad toe jumps and a quad Salchow in my free program, but I started to experience heel pain a week before the competition. I was soon diagnosed with plantar fasciitis, which was related to an open growth plate in my heel, and it was so painful that I couldn't tap my toe pick into the ice for my toe jumps and could only manage one quad toe. I placed eighth in my debut at the senior level at Nationals.

After Nationals, I competed in the World Junior Championships in Estonia, and finished just off the podium, in fourth. I had a few more years of age eligibility to compete at the World Junior Championships. Looking to the next season, I was age-eligible and ready to try and qualify for Senior Worlds.

To help me recover from my plantar fasciitis and prepare for being a senior level competitor, in the summer of 2015 some of the U.S. Figure Skating officials suggested that I start incorporating more strength and conditioning training into my routine. During that off-season I went to the U.S. Olympic & Paralympic Training Center in Colorado Springs. That's where I first met Brandon Siakel, who would become my longtime strength and conditioning coach.

I wasn't really doing much in the weight room at that time—I was fifteen—so Brandon introduced me to strength and conditioning and how building up my body could help with my energy and endurance for training. I spent about a month working with him at the Training Center, and quickly picked up some exercises I could fold into my regular training. He also did a full assessment of my body and identified weak areas that I needed to work on. We focused on increasing the mobility in my ankles and the mechanics of landing jumps so that I was in proper alignment and wouldn't cause unnecessary strain on my joints. He taught me about keeping my trunk in line with my shins and making sure that my knee stayed in line with my middle toes when I landed jumps—things that I still keep in mind today.

That month, we worked together three days a week, setting up my first strength and conditioning program. After I returned to California, Raf immediately noticed a difference in my jumping and called U.S. Figure Skating to have Brandon continue working with me.

For the 2015–16 season, I kept my Michael Jackson short program from the previous season but created a new free program set to Saint-Saëns's Symphony No. 3 with Organ, choreographed by Nikolai Morozov, a well-known coach and choreographer based in New Jersey. He coached Shizuka Arakawa to the 2006 Olympic gold medal. Up to that point all my competition programs were choreographed by my own coaching teams, so I thought it was time to explore different styles of choreography. I decided to fly east for part of the summer to work with Nikolai. I really enjoyed the change of pace and his different perspective on skating, and was pleased with my new program.

That season, I skated well with those programs in the Junior Grand Prix series, winning both my Junior Grand Prix events and the Final, which was in Barcelona, Spain, that season. Before Nationals, Raf brought his skaters to Colorado Springs to train at the World Arena, because he felt we would have more ice time than we were getting during the holiday season at East West Ice Palace. But it was quite crowded at the rink, since it's a popular Olympic training site; and it was difficult to get as much time to play my program music and run through my programs as I wanted. So my mom and I ended up driving around to find other rinks in town to supplement my training time.

With Nationals fast approaching, I was getting anxious about not having enough time to train, and remembering how much I enjoyed working on my programs at Nikolai's rink in New Jersey, I decided to go back there for some consistent training before the National Championships.

Raf and I had a practice at the Air Force Academy rink in Colorado Springs on New Year's Eve, and I remember we had the entire session to ourselves because of the holiday. The practice was at night and we got off the ice right at midnight, New Year's Day. After practice, I told Raf I didn't feel productive training in Colorado and wanted to go to New Jersey to polish my free program with Nikolai. He seemed supportive of my decision. As I remember it, we both said, "We'll see you at Nationals."

My mom and I ended up staying for two weeks in New Jersey, and Nikolai provided exactly the attention to detail on the nontechnical elements that I felt my skating needed.

Injuries continued to plague me and the pain I felt in my left hip had been escalating throughout the season, from a dull, constant ache to sharp pain when I dug my toe pick into the ice to launch into my quad toe. I went to a few different doctors, but they said it wasn't something that I would damage more if I pushed through it. I trusted them, and given my bullheaded theory of training by repetitions ad infinitum, it was a no-brainer to continue forging ahead to Nationals, which were in St. Paul, Minnesota, that year.

At Nationals, I was in a lot of pain through the short and free programs, especially when I tapped my left foot in for the quad toe. But I managed to get through both programs—and became the first to land six quads in a competition in the United States.

In the short program I made a little bobble on two jumps, turning out on the quad Salchow and putting my hand down on the triple Axel, but I became the first skater to land two quad jumps in the short program at U.S. Nationals. In the free program, I fell on the triple Axel but landed four quads, which was another first for the free program, making it six quads in those two programs. Despite the pain, I came in third and was excited to be named to the U.S. teams for the 2016 World Championships and the 2016 World Junior Championships.

After the competition, I got to the exhibition, which was always a more relaxed performance, when the medalists get to skate programs without having to worry about fulfilling the requirements of competitive programs. I decided to include a quad, since that's what everyone was expecting from me. I remember hearing someone yell, "Do a quad!" and thinking, "All right, I guess I will," and launched into the quad toe. As I tapped down on my left skate, I felt my hip give out from under me and I barely lifted off the ice. I was in shock and wasn't sure how I could continue. I decided that I simply couldn't, and grabbed my left hip and tried to skate off, in blinding pain—I know I had an awful grimace on my face as I limped off the ice.

The medical team from U.S. Figure Skating put me in a wheelchair, since I couldn't walk, and took me to the local hospital, where I had an MRI. The doctors told me I had popped my ASIS, or anterior superior iliac spine, where the thigh muscle attaches to the hip. By building up my muscle so much with all the quad jump training, the muscle detached, taking a section of bone with it, also known as an avulsion fracture. I was supposed to compete at both Junior and Senior World Championships that season—it would have been my first Worlds at the senior level—that were scheduled for a month later. But with my injury, I had to withdraw.

The doctor recommended surgery to reattach the muscle to the ASIS, and Peter Zapalo, former Director of Sports Science and Medicine at U.S. Figure Skating, connected me with the medical team at the United States Olympic & Paralympic Committee (USOPC). They helped me to arrange the operation at the University of California at San Diego Medical Center, with Dr. Catherine Robertson.

Dr. Robertson was confident that I would be able to fully recover and get back to where I was before the injury, and Brandon was, too.

But I wasn't so sure. After all, during the season, the doctors my mom and I consulted had told me that the issue I was having was a minor one, that there was little to no chance it would get worse or that I could do more damage if I continued pushing. That was the whole reason why I continued to train. And, of course, that advice turned out to be wrong.

Still, I trusted Brandon, and I didn't have a choice. I was in so much pain and couldn't skate the way I wanted to without the surgery.

After the operation, the doctors put me in a hip brace to stabilize my hip, and I could only walk with crutches. After a few days in the hospital, I asked my mom if I could stay with my uncle, who lived in San Diego with my aunt and cousins Jerome and Kevin Wang. I was feeling really down and lost without skating, and continued to worry about whether I would recover fully, so I thought being with my family would help. My mom and I ended up spending about a week there. She drove me to the beach almost every day and I would hobble on my crutches to sit by the water.

The World Championships were in Boston that year. I was able to attend and watch the competition live, but had some serious pangs of jealousy. I should have been skating out there. I'd believed I had a chance of making the top eight at the senior level, and potentially winning at the junior level, for which I had also qualified. I had really wanted to compete at both, and it was hard to sit in the stands as a spectator. Javier Fernandez of Spain won his second World title, Yuzuru Hanyu earned silver, and Jin Boyang of China won bronze. Watching them, I was both motivated and a little intimidated about how competitive the field was getting.

After the week at my uncle's, the USOPC arranged for me to start physical therapy at its training center in Chula Vista, California. I was behind in my schoolwork, so I caught up in between physical therapy sessions. Having only school to worry about was a welcome change of pace. I enjoyed being a full-time student again so much that it gave me another opportunity to seriously think about where my skating was going and how far I wanted to take it. Up to that point, I had just blindly forged ahead because it was what I was supposed to do. While in Irvine, I had contemplated quitting mainly because I was frustrated with my progress on the ice. But this time, I had the time now to gain a little more perspective and began to see the world outside skating, which seemed just as appealing to me. So while in recovery, being off the ice for what ended up being five months, I entertained the possibility that this might be where my skating ended. If I didn't keep going, I could focus more on school and getting ready to go to college. I wondered if the injury was a sign that skating wasn't the career route for me, so I readied myself mentally to see whether I would be able to recover and progress any further.

Over the next month, I gradually started to feel stronger. Most of my physical therapy was just getting in the pool and walking around very, very gently in the water for about ten to fifteen minutes a day.

After the medical team thought I was ready, I flew to Colorado Springs to finish another couple months of rehab. I was still on crutches, and trying to gradually move more and more of my body. The therapists would move my hips very gently to break down any scar tissue that might be forming, and ask me to activate the muscles I needed to strengthen that hip area. I would squeeze my glutes and my core, then relax them, squeeze them again and release— nothing strenuous, just tedious, gentle exercise.

After a long two weeks of this, I began adding some strength and conditioning moves. Brandon started working on my right leg to keep it toned and then tried to slowly build up my left leg to the point where I could eventually match the weights I was lifting with the right. I wasn't allowed back on the ice until three or four months after the surgery. Even then, the first few weeks I could skate only for five minutes, then eight, then ten, fifteen, and thirty.

Progress was slow, and I was (and am) pretty impatient, so I fast-forwarded just a little. After the first few times I skated, I stayed on the ice a little longer than I was supposed to. I didn't do anything crazy—I wasn't doing any jumps or anything to risk doing more damage after the surgery. But in my mind, I felt the impact and movement from just stroking around were so minimal that there was very, very little risk of doing much harm.

About four and a half months after my surgery, I tried my first jump. And, yes, it was a little earlier than the therapists wanted, but by that point I was lifting weights with both legs and feeling pretty strong. The pain was gone, so I started going for it.

It took another couple of months before I could start training at the same level I had been before the surgery—and Dr. Robertson was right: I made a full recovery. The surgery and physical therapy gave me the chance to think more deeply about skating and the role I wanted it to play in my life. Caught up in the daily grind of training, I had lost sight of why I started skating in the first place, but those first few weeks back on the ice reminded me of how much I loved the sport. And of how much I could still accomplish.

3 "AMERICA'S HOPE"

初生牛犊不怕虎

Newborn calves are not afraid of tigers.

During my final stage of rehab in Colorado Springs, I skated on my own for about a month. I was beginning to get my jumps back; and because I wasn't in pain anymore, I even managed to add two quads—landing the quad flip and quad Lutz, two of the harder jumps in my arsenal. I was really excited about my progress, and wanted to get back to Raf to work with him on refining those jumps and putting them into my programs.

What Raf does better than anyone is finding ways to set up jumps in programs to give me the best chances of landing them cleanly and consistently, and now I had two more quads to work with. But I also knew those two were so new that I needed to continue developing them with his help to make sure my technique was on the right track. Raf was the only person I trusted when it came to my technique—no one could compare with him from a technical standpoint. So I was curious to see what he would do now that I had these two additional elements.

My mom and I drove from Colorado Springs to Los Angeles—well, actually I drove the entire way and my mom rode shotgun. I had just gotten my license and I really wanted to drive as much as I could. And I couldn't wait to get back to the rink and see Raf.

By this time, he was coaching at Lakewood ICE in Lakewood, California. For a while, my mom and I stayed in San Diego with my uncle and aunt. But the drive from there meant we spent four or five hours a day on the freeway. After about three weeks, we rented an apartment in Irvine.

The first time back at the rink, I excitedly showed Raf my two new jumps, expecting him to be impressed. Even if he was, it was overshadowed by frustration. He was still upset that I had tried the quad in the exhibition after Nationals—he thought it was an unnecessary risk—and he told me I was not smart for doing so. And he was right. Raf is still convinced that some of my injuries, in particular the avulsion injury that required surgery, occurred because I was being too ambitious in training. He would say in his hallmark way, "If you need to jump over a hole that is bigger than you are capable of jumping over, would you just jump in and die? Or would you train to jump over a smaller hole, and every day increase the size of the hole until you can safely make it across?" I know he was frustrated by my injuries because he wanted to keep forging ahead with his vision for my skating. Whenever I got hurt, I'd have to take time off to recover, so it would be a setback not just for me but for him as well.

He seemed glad to see that I was able to learn new elements but was still critical of my training approach. That surprised me because I thought I had been putting in good work and hadn't wasted time, despite my surgery and rehab. It was important for me to show him that I was still competitive and strong and ready to work again. I thought being able to land two new jumps would be evidence of that.

Raf wasn't convinced. He knew that he had prepared me to land the two elements. However, he had a plan for how he wanted me to progress through the different quad jumps and for how to keep building on them until I could do what no skater had tried before: landing six quad jumps in a free program. Early that season, I skated in a small summer competition and had performed my two new elements. Raf again thought that was not smart of me and felt I had rushed things.

He likes to keep his plan close to his vest, and he wanted to wait another year before unleashing all my quads on the world. The following year, 2017, would be the one before the 2018 Olympics, and he felt that season would be the right time to incrementally build my elements up to peak at the Games in South Korea. Plus, he didn't want to always reveal to other competitors exactly what I was capable of doing: he didn't want to put all our cards on the table and give them the opportunity to train similar elements and jump layouts.

I disagreed and wanted to get as much experience with my two new elements as possible. I hoped that these two new quad jumps would make me more competitive—in the United States for sure but perhaps even in the world. I knew it wasn't a straight line to becoming a top-tier skater internationally. My strategy counted on having a high base value for my programs, owing to my difficult jumps; but even with two new quads, I wasn't sure it would be enough. I had finished third at the U.S. championships, after landing six quad jumps. Would adding two more make a difference in my standing? I didn't really confess this new worry to Raf, and that might have led to some tension between us. As my confidence started to falter, I started to disengage from him. Again, it all boiled down to communication; and neither of us was really listening or opening up to the other.

After the 2016 Nationals, I received feedback from judges and officials at U.S. Figure Skating that, while my jumps were getting attention, my skating was lacking in program components. That's the part of your score that focuses more on the art of skating and things like the quality of your edges, the power of your skating, how well the elements and the music go together, and how much energy and emotion a program has. The bottom-line message was that I needed to improve the artistic side of my skating.

I agreed with the judges and officials. With my approach of tackling things one at a time, I had so far focused on bringing my technical abilities to as high a level as I could. Now it was time to pay more attention to the program component side of my skating.

In May 2016, while I was still doing rehab in Colorado Springs, I started contemplating working with a new choreographer to really improve the artistic side of my skating. My mom and I considered several big-name choreographers, most notably Marina Zoueva. Marina is an excellent coach and choreographer who coached mostly ice dancers, including several Olympic medalists—2010 and 2018 Olympic Gold medalists Tessa Virtue and Scott Moir, 2014 Olympic Gold medalists Meryl Davis and Charlie White, and 2018 Olympic Bronze medalists Maia Shibutani and Alex Shibutani. I asked her if she could help me choreograph my short program and she agreed. So I visited her base in Canton, Michigan, to work on my new short program to the music from the ballet *Le Corsaire* for a week and returned to Colorado Springs to continue my rehab.

Back in California, my worry that my skating abilities would never be enough to make me truly competitive continued to grow. As my confidence waned, my jumps started to get less consistent.

Fearing that my cycle of self-doubt would get worse, my mom and I decided I needed a change of setting. With the knowledge that components should be at the top of our mind, we decided to turn, just as I had the year before, to my choreographer.

Marina's coaching team included Oleg Epstein, Johnny Johns, Massimo Scali, and Yelena Sokolova. And after spending a few days with her team over the summer, I knew I needed a lengthier stay there. I arrived in Canton in September, and I immediately thought, "This is a great training environment." At the time, Patrick Chan from Canada had moved to Canton to work with Marina as well. Patrick was a three-time world champion and a silver medalist from the

2014 Olympics, and was training for his third Games. I really liked the positivity there. Even if I was having a really bad jumping day, I got something out of it; somehow even those rough days felt productive there. Marina paid attention to every little detail, from the exact location on my blade where I put my body weight, to what colors my costume was, to every facial expression I made on the ice. I started the day working on jumps in my first session and then moved on to refining my programs and presentation during the next two practices with Marina and her coaching team. During the competition season, we had simulated competitions on Thursday and Friday, during which we would have a six-minute warm-up and perform our programs wearing our costumes, just like during actual events.

Because Marina and her team mostly worked with ice dance teams, my mom was a little doubtful before we went to Canton about how much ice time I would get and about how the coaches would navigate having Patrick and me, who jumped, skate alongside ice dancers who didn't. Fortunately, we quickly got used to the different skating patterns in the rink, and did our jumps next to the ice dancers without any problem. As we trained together, Patrick became like an older brother to me. While I was little intimidated at first to train next to him, he was immediately friendly and warm and made me feel welcome. Even when we weren't training, he would try to look after me and take me on food runs in his sports car.

And it wasn't just Patrick who was welcoming. Everyone was supportive and always trying to help one another. I remember Charlie White and Alex Shibutani even tried to help me with my triple Axel because I was having so much trouble with it. Their perspective was refreshing because they weren't trying to teach me technique—they were looking at the jump logically, pointing out what looked unnatural to them and suggesting other movements to try. To my surprise, it kind of helped.

Working with ice dancers, who focus so much on presentation and making very precise movements on the ice, helped me to better understand the intricacy of what a complete skating program could, and should, be. Taking this next step to improve my skating components was motivating for me. It was refreshing to switch my point of view and not be so laser focused on jumps. Accepting that there was another, equally important aspect to skating made me realize that I didn't have to put all my worth as a skater on whether I could land jumps consistently or not. Working on those things was really what I needed at that time to bring my skating to the next level, so I could start showing the judges I was more than just a jumper. In the fall of 2016, with Marina as my coach, I skated in the first event of my first senior Grand Prix series, Trophée de France. I was naturally nervous to be warming up and competing on the same ice as Javier Fernandez and Denis Ten, with whom I had trained briefly at Lake Arrowhead. I was also worried that there would be an awkward moment with Raf, because Adam Rippon, who also trained with Raf in California, was competing as well. Since Raf and I hadn't really cleared the air about my spending so much time with Marina, I feared seeing him at the Grand Prix would be a little uncomfortable.

When I saw him at the rink, I asked Marina: "I don't know how I should act around him. Should I talk to him?" She suggested that I say hello but not to get too caught up in thought about it, since I had to focus on the competition. I gathered my courage and went up to him to say hi. To my relief, he didn't seem upset—things between us felt okay.

I didn't skate well at that competition. I skated a clean short program with a quad Lutz and a triple toe combination, a quad flip, and a double Axel, but had a shakier free program with falls on my quad toe and quad Salchow. I had planned on executing five quads but only landed two of them cleanly. I finished fourth, just missing a medal.

Two weeks later, as I was training for my next Grand Prix event, the NHK Trophy in Sapporo, Japan, I realized I still really needed help with my jumps. While I felt stronger performance-wise, I couldn't get my jump consistency back. So, I ended up asking Raf, a day before I had to leave for Japan, if he could help me out. I told him I was sorry for how things had unfolded and that I still needed his help and hoped that he would take me back. I was a little nervous about how he would respond, but it was just what he wanted to hear. He welcomed me back. There was no drama, and no awkwardness between us because of our time apart. As Raf saw it, I was like his skating son. If I went away and needed to work things out for myself and realize he could still help me, then he wouldn't turn me away or refuse to give me support.

It's all about balance. With so much focus on the skating skills and presentation of my programs, my jumps took a back seat. After not working with Raf for a few months, my technique had started to falter a little bit. I tried to work out the kinks myself. My toe and Salchow were okay, and the flip and Lutz were getting stronger. But I couldn't land these elements together consistently in programs, and my Axel was still pretty unreliable. I didn't want things to continue going downward. Without high technical content, I wouldn't be competitive, no matter how good the rest of my program was. I needed to go back to Raf.

It wouldn't be the first time I made such an adjustment, as my skating career has taken these pendulum swings between being focused on technical skills and presentation elements. As a young skater, I started with weaker technical ability and concentrated on simultaneously developing my skating skills more. After I worked with Raf, my technical elements took priority. After I worked with Marina, the quality of my skating skills and presentation improved. But my jumps naturally got a little weaker. So I went back to Raf, armed with a deeper appreciation for how to capitalize on the non-jumping parts of my programs. Every time I went to a new place or started working with a new coach, I was absorbing everything that they had to offer me; each had something very valuable to contribute that I've tried to maintain in my skating to this day.

No matter what, Raf was still the expert when it came to technique: no one could break down the mechanics behind a jump like he could. After so many years of experience in the sport, he used some new strategies in teaching me the quads that he hadn't really put together in a comprehensive way for any other student before. Raf compared it to the Fosbury Flop, the famous revolutionary technique in high jump that Dick Fosbury from the United States debuted at the 1968 Summer Olympics in Mexico City. Until then, high jumpers either straddled the bar or rolled over it facing forward. Fosbury, a bioengineer, figured out that a jumper could maintain a lower center of gravity and not leap as high but still pull himself over the bar if he pushed off facing backward and flipped over the bar on his back, arching to avoid touching it. The strategy earned Fosbury an Olympic gold, and completely changed the sport of high jump.

Raf wanted to do the same for men's figure skating. I was his guinea pig, which was fine with me because I had complete faith in his prowess in teaching jumps.

I grew up learning a European-based technique, which is a little different from the way jumps are taught in the United States. My technique is heavily dependent on body position in preparation for takeoffs, angling and twisting my torso in such a way to generate torque. If you're doing a double, you need to rotate upon your axis by about twenty-five degrees in order to get the rotations in. When you're doing triple jumps, you rotate upon that axis by another twenty-five degrees. For quads, you need to rotate by another twenty-five degrees. Basically you're pushing yourself more and more to one side—the right side in my case—in order to gain torque;

similar to a bow and arrow, the farther you pull the bowstring the farther the arrow will shoot.

My first real jumping coach, Karel Kovar, and Jozef Sabovčik had trained in Czechoslovakia, so that's two European coaches. After Karel, I started working with Akop Manoukian and then with Genia Chernyshova, both of whose techniques were Russian-based.

After coaching some successful junior skaters from Russia while in Armenia, Raf was invited to coach in Russia as an assistant to legendary coach Tatiana Tarasova, who coached more skaters to Olympic gold than any other coach in history—an incredible eight gold medals. Before starting with Raf, because I'd trained with so many European coaches, I knew that Raf's technique would work perfectly for me. After my time with Marina, he picked up right where we had left off, and continued with his plan for preparing me for the 2018 Games.

Raf went with me to the Grand Prix in Japan, where I skated against Yuzuru Hanyu for the first time. That was a surreal experience; he had won gold at the 2014 Olympics and was a favorite for repeating as Olympic champion in 2018. I knew he would be among the skaters I would potentially have to face if I were to make it to PyeongChang. At the time I was just excited to finally be skating on the same ice as Yuzuru, after missing my chance to compete at Worlds because of my surgery. I tried not to get too distracted, but I continued to struggle with my jumps and my two performances weren't as clean as they could have been. But given my high technical content, I managed to finish second, behind Yuzuru. It was my first international medal as a senior skater and I was beginning to feel that I might just belong in this new, rarefied world of athletes.

It was especially meaningful because up to that point, my mom had not traveled with me to an international competition. Knowing she had never been to Japan after giving up her chance to study there, my siblings and I chipped in to get her a plane ticket so she could watch me skate.

My results from those two events qualified me for the Grand Prix Final, a competition in which only the top six skaters of the Grand Prix series from each discipline—women's, men's, ice dance, and pairs—are invited to compete. The final was held in Marseille, France, in December 2016. Again, my performance wasn't perfect, but I skated well enough to earn silver behind Yuzuru.

After the Grand Prix Final, my mom and I returned to California so I could continue training with Raf. We had given up our previous lease, so we stayed at a few Airbnbs until we found a small apartment in Long Beach a few miles from the Lakewood rink.

I had gathered more momentum as the season wore on, and my performances were getting stronger. I was more confident in my abilities, and I was even feeling bold enough to add a fifth quad in my free program at Nationals in Kansas City, Missouri, in January 2017.

I landed two clean quads in the short program, the quad Lutz triple toe combination, and the quad flip, along with the triple Axel. As was typical of my mindset at the time, I figured I should just go for broke in the free program and attempt five quads, including four different ones. That time, the risk actually paid off. I won my first senior National title!

After my fifth quad, NBC commentator Tara Lipinski said, "This is ridiculous!" and fellow commentator Johnny Weir called me "America's hope, Nathan Chen." They were of course also dropping heavy hints about the likelihood that I would be competing the next year at the Olympics in PyeongChang, South Korea.

The intensity of attention only increased with the ISU Four Continents competition, which was held in Gangneung, South Korea, in the same venue that would host the Olympic skating events. I actually hated hearing this commentary, because I felt I hadn't fully proved myself yet, but it did give me a boost of confidence and I felt the most in control of my jumps at that event that I had in my career. I again landed two quads in my short program and five quads in my free.

That competition brought me another first: I was the first skater to land five quads in a free skate at an international competition.

All that set me up for what could have been another podium finish at the World Championships in Helsinki, Finland. It was my first senior World Championships, and I was on the hunt for another win after Nationals and Four Continents. I added another quad—the flip, in combination with a double toe—to my free program. But I fell on two of them and finished sixth.

I couldn't hide my disappointment after I skated and I know I grimaced after hitting my final pose. I knew I had the ability to land that program. Ability and consistency are two different things, and I needed to figure out how to properly train my body and mind to accomplish my goals. I had a lot left to learn.

4 DREAD

失败是成功之母

Failure is the mother of success.

It wasn't just inexperience that got the best of me at that World Championships. During the second half of the 2017 season, I had begun to feel a deep pinching pain in my hips, especially in my right hip. So, after Worlds, I went back to the doctors at the USOPC. They ordered an MRI that revealed a new injury: femoroacetabular impingement (FAI) and labrum tears in both hips. It's a common injury among athletes, especially skaters who jump, which puts a lot of strain on the hip joint. The labrum is the cartilage that rings the hip socket where the thigh bone meets the hip and acts like a rubber seal to hold the thigh bone in place. When the labrum tears, the joint becomes unstable, straining the muscles, leading to pain in the hip or groin, which I felt.

Not surprisingly, the doctors said it was exacerbated by the constant strain from all the quad jumps I trained. If I'm standing and I raise my right knee in front of me like an "h," it's painful to move my heel to the right or rotate my hip internally. But I need to make that internal hip rotation for the Axel and Salchow jumps. And even for the other jumps, the torque I generate on takeoff and the landings on my right leg put a lot of pressure on my hip. At its best, it just feels stiff and I don't have full range of motion in rotating the leg in the hip joint. At its worst, I can feel grinding in the joint and I lose strength and stability. While I'm training, I end up trying to compensate for that weakness with my adductor and hip flexors, which strains those muscles, so it's like a domino effect of damage and pain. And, of course, the pain usually increases at the worst possible time—just before and during competitions—because I dial up the volume of repetitions I do to get prepared. Which just aggravates the injury.

That summer, the USOPC sports medicine team sent me to see Dr. Marc Philippon, an orthopedic surgeon and hip specialist in Vail, Colorado, who worked with a lot of athletes with this injury. He told me that surgery was an option, but I was reluctant to have another operation for a couple of reasons. I knew surgery would correct my root cause of the injury, and manage the pain, but I was also afraid that with the time I needed for recovery, I wouldn't be able to train properly. On top of that, I worried the surgery would potentially change my jump technique too much—not something I wanted to risk with the Olympics just eight months away.

The other option Dr. Philippon gave me were injections of platelet rich plasma, or PRP. It's a regenerative medicine therapy that uses my own blood cells to jump-start healing in muscles, tendons, ligaments, and joints. He would take a few tubes of blood from me and then centrifuge them to separate out the platelets, which contain growth factors. Those platelets would be injected into my hip area, using ultrasound to target the places where the labrum was the most torn. The growth factors and other cellular components that are good for soft tissue injuries like I had would help to rebuild and protect the muscles, tendons, and ligaments that were straining to compensate for the labrum tears. Most importantly, they could reduce the pain I felt and help me to rely less on anti-inflammatory drugs and even avoid steroids.

Dr. Philippon was pretty confident PRP would get me through the coming Olympic season, starting on July 1, 2017, with the Olympics in February. But there was a catch: I would have to fly to Vail and spend a day to get my blood cells extracted, prepared, and injected. Then I would need a night before I could walk comfortably. And after that, I would have to take it easy for about a week once I was back home before I could really push myself and train aggressively.

Still, it was my best option. Since it was the off-season, I got the first treatment. It helped a lot but it didn't have the lasting effect that I was hoping for. I went on tour and was soon hurting again, so I went back to Vail for another treatment. The second time, it lasted much longer, so I got a third injection during the middle of the season to help get me through the most intense part of training, and, hopefully, the Olympics.

Even with the PRP, I needed to dial down the intensity of my training every time I started to feel pain. Constantly pounding on my hip by practicing jump after jump nearly every day aggravated the injury. Rest helped, but that was the last thing I felt I could do during such a critical season.

Since I started working with Brandon Siakel, and throughout the recovery after my surgery in 2016, he had talked to me about paying more attention to calibrating my training in order to relieve some of that physical pressure on my body. The idea was not to train less but to train more efficiently, and vary the volume of jumps I did on different days of the week.

I trusted his expertise, but I had gotten this far with my tried-and-true training methods and I didn't feel it was the right time to make major changes in my routine. In my effort to improve my jumps, I continued attempting them, until I was confident that I could land them consistently.

Brandon tried to emphasize that being more flexible with my training might help me to get more out of each session. He would come to California and try to help me measure my training load and come up with ways of helping me to calibrate that: having high-volume days at the start of the week, a lower-volume day in the middle of the week, and high-volume days at the end of the week and making sure I wasn't doing the same high-level training every single day. We used formulas, like rating how much I exerted myself on the ice during a session from one to ten, and multiplying that measure by how long the session was to come up with some metrics for how much energy I was exerting and, indirectly, how much strain my body was feeling. But ultimately, those were subjective measures and we didn't even know if they were actually reliable metrics for much of what I was doing. I also feel that although I understood what Brandon was trying to do by having me vary the volume of my training more, when things weren't going well, I would resort to the only thing I thought would give me the confidence I needed in my jumps—training hard with repetition after repetition.

Raf also tried to change my mentality, but I still believed I needed those additional repetitions. Adjusting that mindset was something I had to learn on my own—and would, in fact, take another few years. At the time, I thought it was impossible to learn quads and put multiple different types of quads in a program without pushing past pain and pushing past my comfort zone. That's what athletes always do. You can't just wake up one day and do it. But I had to learn, the hard way, to find the right balance between that drive and listening to my body.

Starting the 2017–18 season, which culminated in the Winter Games in PyeongChang, I was also dealing with an entirely new type of pressure. Because of my wins the year before, people were starting to mention me as an up-and-coming favorite for winning an Olympic medal, if not gold. I knew I was just one of many who had a reasonable chance for that gold. Raf thought it was realistic that I could earn a medal in PyeongChang and that I might even have a chance at gold. I was doing things in my programs that not many skaters had attempted before, both with the number of quads and the variety of quad jumps I did. I don't know exactly when people started calling me "Quad King," but it must have been around that time. I thought it was funny but also a bit over-the-top.

It's not that I didn't enjoy the fact that people considered me a medal contender. I just didn't know how to handle the pressure. As I got closer to that goal, that praise only amplified the worry that I would fall short of everyone else's expectations. My excitement was starting to turn into fear.

I started getting big sponsors, like Bridgestone, Coca-Cola, Kellogg's, Nike, and later, United Airlines. I had begun working with an agent, Yuki Saegusa, from IMG, in 2016; and Yuki helped me to navigate all the great opportunities that I was presented with. One of them included collaborating with the fashion designer Vera Wang, who had been a skater herself and had designed some iconic costumes for skaters like Nancy Kerrigan, Michelle Kwan, and Evan Lysacek.

I met Vera in New York and we immediately hit it off. I had admired the outfits she had created for other skaters and knew that she had a good understanding of what made a figure skating costume—one that would be durable and not get in the way of the physical demands of a program but that was unique and reflected the character of the program. She showed me some pieces she had made for Evan, and that was very cool. My mom had made most of my costumes when I was younger, and I had worked with some costume designers in the past but never with a team that was on this level. I trusted Vera to take the creative lead. My only request was that I be comfortable in the outfit, which she made a top priority.

The first costume she designed for me was the outfit I wore at U.S. Nationals in January 2018; my free program costume was a very contemporary, sleek black outfit with a silver zipper running down the back. With her experience, she really understood where a costume needed to be reinforced and how fabric might shift while I did spins and jumps. I've never had costumes that were of such high quality, and I'm so appreciative of all the care and attention Vera and her team put into each one. She had a tailor's dummy made to my measurements in her studio so her team could create costumes even if I couldn't be there for every fitting, which was really helpful for me.

Along with the sponsors and opportunities to work with talent like Vera, I was also getting much more media attention. NBC began focusing on me a lot more, and I received tons of interview requests where I had to talk about myself. I didn't have much experience dealing with the media, so it was all new to me. I just wanted to focus on improving my skating instead of talking about my progress.

I also didn't like revealing which elements I was planning on doing at upcoming competitions—which quads, and how many—but of course that's all everyone asked me. This was something that Raf and I agreed on. He wasn't exactly secretive, but he didn't like revealing my jump layouts, because he knew other skaters would try to match them.

I finally learned to just say, "I don't know. We'll see what happens." All the attention, and the added obligation of doing press, made me anxious. Reporters were asking me about my strategy going into the Games, trying to get any kind of information out of me and putting questions into my head that I had never even thought about—like how I expected to feel at the Games and how I was dealing with the pressure of competing in my first Olympics. All their questions only reinforced for me the high stakes of my situation.

When I was alone, those questions would come swirling back in my mind, and I would wonder, "What will the Games be like? How will I feel?" And then, "How can I do this?" I worried about letting my team down. I felt that there were so many expectations being asked of me and I hadn't even won a World medal yet. I started questioning whether I had what it takes.

I shouldn't have spent so much energy on those distractions, because doing so didn't benefit me in practice or help me in my training. Back then, I didn't know it was something I needed to address and manage; and even if I had known that, I wouldn't have known how. I just thought bearing the weight of all that expectation was part of my responsibility as an Olympic hopeful. The more anxious I got, the more frustrated I began to feel on the ice when practices didn't go well.

And as the season went on, I think the pressure amplified some of the bad habits I had, like losing control of my emotions when I felt stressed. During any training session, there are usually several skaters working on their programs at the same time; and when a skater's program music plays, there's an unspoken rule that other skaters try to keep out of their way and give that skater priority as they set up their jumps and use the entire sheet of ice for their run-through. Once during that season, I was really irritated by the fact that I couldn't land one of my jumps, and I saw my friend Michal Březina, a Czech skater who also worked with Raf, skating by. I popped the jump and yelled at him for getting in the way and breaking my concentration, even though he hadn't. I was just taking my anger out on him. I knew I was in the wrong, so I went over to him afterward and apologized, and he was very understanding; he said he could tell I was on edge that entire season.

Another of my good friends at the rink, Romain Ponsart, who is from France but trained with Raf beginning in 2016, also helped me through those challenging times. Romain was a six-time French national medalist, and easygoing enough to tolerate my frequent bouts of frustration with my skating at that time. He lived a block away from me, and provided a much-needed social outlet for me away from training. We challenged each other on the ice as well; he could also do a triple Axel, quad Salchow, and quad toe; so we played a game in which we each had three attempts to land those jumps and whoever landed more of them won. I would go over to his place to watch TV on the weekends, or we'd walk around Long Beach. I remember that after one particularly bad practice of mine before the Olympics, he pulled me aside and said that I needed a mental break. We went to the mall and relaxed for the rest of the day; I must admit that helped a lot.

But there was no denying that anxiety was starting to seep into every aspect of my preparation that season. I was assigned to skate in the 2017 Grand Prix events in the fall, Rostelecom Cup in Moscow in October and Skate America in Lake Placid, New York, a month later. While I was practicing for the Rostelecom Cup, I was trying to get through the elements and I kept falling and falling and falling. I went to Raf and told him I didn't know what was happening and I didn't know how to fix whatever was going wrong. He gave me corrections, and I made them, but continued to fall. Even if I did manage to land a few jumps, I had to fight to do so and I didn't see how I could skate strong programs when I was so fatigued from fighting so hard to make each and every element work. I just couldn't get the repetitions I needed to boost my confidence and my training wasn't consistent at all. That would be a pattern for the rest of that important season. I would struggle with jumps, fall or pop them, which would make me more anxious. I was so focused on trying to execute each element perfectly that even if I did succeed in landing a jump, I would continue to dwell on the missed jumps and the mistakes I had made, almost obsessively, which only chipped away further at my confidence.

I managed to win both Grand Prix events, which meant I qualified for the Grand Prix Final. I went on to win my first Grand Prix Final that December, 2017. Still, I had felt I hadn't reached the skating standard that I had set for myself at any of those three Grand Prix events that season. I comparatively skated the best at Rostelecom, but I still made a bunch of mistakes. I leaned really far forward in the landings on my quad flip and the triple Axel in the short program, and in the free program I popped a quad toe and I didn't land my two triple Axels really well. At Skate America I also made a couple of errors—again with the triple Axel in the short program, when I slid off my takeoff edge but still managed to pull off the jump. Then in the free program, I stepped out of my quad flip and fell on my quad toe. At the Grand Prix Final, I landed all three of my elements in the short program, but popped a quad Salchow and fell on a quad toe late in the free program.

With each competition, as I got closer to the Olympics, there was more attention focused on me. With every skate, I became even more aware of all the eyes on me, all the attention and all the interviews I had to do.

In order to land quads, I need to be confident that my body can physically handle the training and the repetitions of all those jumps. If I'm not able to physically be at the level I need to be to attempt a quad, my mind blocks out and essentially tells my body, "Don't attempt this jump because you will hurt yourself." That led me to either bail out of the jump and pop it, or fall in really unpredictable ways. That conflict only amplifies when I'm feeling stressed or frustrated, but I tried to stop listening to my brain and push through anyway. I was taught by most of the coaches I worked with to fight through any and all physical or mental hurdles I encountered in practice so that I could develop the resilience to power through them if they occurred during competitions. Encountering these issues during competition was something I was especially afraid of, since I still wasn't quite sure how to overcome them. My only strategy was to try to reject the mental barrier, thinking, "Stop being weak, go for it." Ultimately, that approach didn't work as well as I would have liked. And it was risky because it raised the chances that I would get injured.

Brandon Siakel could see the spiral I was descending into, and he was concerned about the toll it would eventually take on my body. To help me analyze the intensity of my practices, he began keeping track of the number of jumps I did in each session, so we could go back and figure out how many jumps was too many before my hip injury started flaring up again. But with the mentality I had at the time, I wouldn't stop until I was satisfied with my technique, and that was often way past the threshold we came up with. Because it was the internal rotation that aggravated the injury, I felt the most pain when I launched into the triple Axel and quad Salchow. But those are the jumps I struggle with the most, so my approach that season was to practice them until I could execute enough successful repetitions. Unfortunately, that came at the price of my hips hurting too much for me to continue. I then had to take a few days off and not work on them until I felt better again. This ended up resulting in less training time in terms of total hours I spent working on these jumps.

The thing is, when you're training quads, you can't just go full steam ahead and do dozens of each type of quad jump every single day, like you can with triples. You're going to break down at some point in time; your body just won't be able to handle it. Instead, you have to find and maintain just the right cadence of jump volume. But in preparing for the 2018 Olympics, I couldn't find that rhythm. I couldn't abandon an element if I wasn't able to land it. I had to keep trying until I was satisfied I could perform it well.

I was so motivated, since the Olympics were the shining prize at the end, that I didn't care how tired I was. This was my dream—it was everything I had ever wanted from my skating. So instead of realizing that I needed to make my practices more intentional, both physically and mentally, I kept my focus on repetition and practicing my jumps again and again and again and again.

I felt strongly that in order to put myself in the best position to win, I needed to capitalize on my strength, which was my technical ability. And I needed to have the highest-scoring technical program in order to stand apart from my competitors. In a sport that is judged, and in which scores reflect a certain amount of subjective variability, I felt that the only objective thing I could control was having the highest base value, or combination of elements that provided the highest possible technical score if I executed them all well. The quad Lutz has the highest base value—13.60 points—of all the jumps I can land. If I landed it in the second half of the program, I would earn an extra 10 percent bonus, for 14.95 points. Throughout the Grand Prix competitions, I started with a quad Lutz–triple toe combination in my short and my free programs, knowing that this would pull in as close to the maximum number of points I could earn. I then added a second quad Lutz in the second half of my free program at Skate America and at the Grand Prix Final that season because I was planning to add it in my Olympic program and wanted to be prepared for how much energy I needed to pull that off.

Because of that, I trained the quad Lutz a lot. It's a jump that requires me to bend my left ankle deeply outward in order to set me up for the outside edge takeoff, and the same jump that injured my ankle back in my years at the Junior level. Gradually, with all the strain I put on my ankle, it became too painful for me to keep practicing that jump.

This meant that the only jump I could really practice consistently was the quad toe, and the rest I really didn't feel confident about. At the National Championships in 2018 in San Jose, which was also the final qualifying competition for the U.S. Olympic team, I couldn't include the Lutz in my programs because of how badly I had injured my ankle. And that played a role in what happened a month later when I tried it at the Olympics. It was the first jump in my short program, and when I couldn't land it, that affected the rest of the program. Often, when I hit the first jump, it sets up a nice flow for the rest of the program. But when I miss the first jump, I waste a lot of energy trying to recover and it becomes challenging to regain that flow.

At Nationals, I knew that there were three spots on the U.S. Olympic men's team. Almost everyone, including me, expected that I could earn one of them. Given my injuries, I didn't skate the programs that I had competed earlier in the season, or the ones I was hoping to skate at the Olympics. But I won the national title. Although that didn't guarantee me a spot on the 2018 Olympic team based on the U.S. Figure Skating Olympic team selection procedures, the national win and my results at the 2017 ISU World Championships (sixth), 2017 Grand Prix series (two gold medals) and Final (first), and 2017 Four Continents Championships (first) earned me one of the spots on the U.S. Olympic team.

I was finally an Olympian, something I had dreamed about since I first started skating on that Olympic training rink back in Salt Lake City.

I remember walking out of the San Jose arena with my sisters. They were so excited that I was an Olympian, asking me how I felt. I recall trying to match their energy and telling them I was excited. My dream had finally come true. And yet I didn't feel the way I thought I would after all those years of striving for this goal and finally achieving it.

Instead, I felt dread.

All I could think was, "Oh no, how am I going to do this? It's the freaking Olympics." The task ahead of me was daunting. I worried about whether I could prepare myself in time, and worried about whether I could perform the way I, my family, Raf, and now the growing team around me expected me to perform. If the Olympics were held that day, I felt I was nowhere near ready to compete well. I held on to the desperate hope that I would feel more confident after training for another three weeks or so until the Games began. Instead of going to the Games with the perspective that I would gain incredible experience as an Olympian and focus on doing my best, I went in with the mentality that I absolutely, positively had to win. So many people had helped me to get to that point, and I had benefited from the support of so many, that I began to feel all that responsibility to succeed start to descend on my shoulders. I couldn't let them down.

In a sense, that can be a good mindset for a competitor to have. And some people thrive under that type of pressure. But I started to crumble. "Oh no, I don't know how to handle this," I thought. In interviews, I said what everyone says when they make the Olympic team, about how happy I was to realize my dream after so many years. Don't get me wrong, I was honored by the chance to represent the United States at the Olympics. I just wasn't sure if I was going to be ready for it now that the moment was fast approaching.

Part of the pressure came from the few wins I had at my competitions that season and the one before. Winning those competitions set up the idea in my mind that I could win in PyeongChang. Up until that point, I had been chasing and chasing this dream of competing against the best skaters and winning. And now that I had done that, the media, my team, and even I suddenly believed that I had caught up. I was scared this would be my one and only chance to win.

In some ways, I reacted like all of us instinctively do when we come too close to a hot surface—we pull away. Even though I had wanted to compete at the Olympics my whole life, now that the chance was no longer a dream but a reality, I didn't know if I had it in me to be the Olympic athlete I had always wanted to be.

People on my team, including my mom and the folks at U.S. Figure Skating, tried to help me navigate the growing pressures by suggesting I speak to other Olympians about how they managed their own journeys to the Games. And I did get great advice from Charlie White and Evan Lysacek, who were very generous in sharing what they had gone through at their respective Games. But everyone's experience is so different, and I had such strong beliefs in what I felt worked for me when it came to training. They could tell me everything about how they navigated the pressure and the expectations, and how they structured their training, but we all prioritize things differently.

In the month between Nationals and the 2018 Games, my stress was at an all-time high. Within my team of Raf, my mom, Brandon, and me, we wanted to find the perfect steps to take, but there was no algorithm to follow. We didn't have the opportunity to attempt varying training plans by trial and error, so we continued to do what had worked in the past. I just had no idea what to expect at the Olympics and could not have predicted how mentally overwhelming the experience would be. I didn't know then that it wasn't only about how technically prepared I was, or how much time I had to train for my first Games. So all I could do was keep doing what I had been doing—which ultimately didn't work.

So, I continued to train full steam ahead, trying to block out the increasing frustration I felt when practices didn't go well. My mantra going into that first Olympics was "Olympic gold or bust." I was going to win, and I wouldn't let myself think about anything else. If I couldn't win Olympic gold, I thought, what was I worth?

The volume of training I did just before the Olympics was probably a lot higher than it should have been. A lot of athletes talk about tapering just before a competition, to make sure they are in peak condition and not too exhausted; in retrospect, I should have done something similar.

Brandon struggled with how insistent he should be in urging me to vary my training intensity, because he, Raf, my mom, and I were really in uncharted waters when it came to training for programs that had not just one but several quadruple jumps, and not just one type of quad but many. No one had really skated these types of programs before. Figuring out how much training was enough and how much was too much, plus factoring in my hip injury, was all new. Brandon watched me at the practice sessions at Nationals in San Jose, where I was having trouble with my triple Axel and just hammering that jump over and over and over again, and falling over and over and over again. He was worried that I was pushing past a very high volume of jumps that might aggravate my hip, but at the same time, he didn't feel it would help if he stepped in and interrupted my training flow just days before the final opportunity to qualify for the Olympics—one of the most important National Championships of my life. At that point, everyone on my team was walking on eggshells around me, and came to the same conclusion: "If it isn't broken, don't fix it." We just didn't know that my mindset, along with my approach to training, was breaking down both my body and mind.

The sense of dread I felt after being named to the Olympic team didn't go away, as I had hoped it would, but instead grew in the month leading up to PyeongChang. Throughout that season, I felt like Sisyphus rolling that boulder up the hill, only to have it roll back down again. I was using all my strength to will it back up in an endless cycle of exhausting, and what felt like futile, effort.

Without the perspective to see the damage I was inflicting on myself, when my training wasn't consistent, I started to blame external factors: it must have been my boots, or it must have been the ice, or it must have been the environment. Everything seemed chaotic and uncertain, which only added to my anxiety as the Olympics approached.

One of the biggest uncertainties had to do with my short program. That entire season, Raf and I were on different pages about the jump layout. Given my ankle injury, he and I went back and forth over what jump layout I should follow in the short program. He didn't want me to do the quad Lutz–triple toe combination and quad Flip, because my injury prevented me from landing the Lutz consistently. He thought the quad Flip–triple toe and quad toe would be more reliable, knowing that at the Olympics, my adrenaline would be kicking in and it would be harder to control the timing of my jumps, especially if they hadn't been consistent in recent weeks. Raf also thought that opting for the easier program layout would be the safer and stronger strategy, because he knew that since I was planning on including six quads in my free program, I had a fighting chance of winning with a good score in the free program even if I didn't place first after the short program. The quad Lutz–triple toe was worth more points, however, so of course I wanted to go for that jump, even though it was riskier than the quad toe–triple toe.

I let my fear of having too low a technical score without the quad Lutz dominate my thinking; I convinced myself that I needed the quad Lutz in order to be competitive. It was the same strategy that propelled me to win at Four Continents the previous season, where being in the lead after the short program ended up providing me enough points to win overall. I thought that if I again maximized my points in the short program, I would have a higher chance of winning after my two program scores were combined. Raf disagreed.

My resolution, such as it was, was to train two different versions of my short program heading into the Olympics. I planned to skate the easier version, which Raf favored, in the team event, which was the first time I would be competing on Olympic ice, and then see how practices went before the men's individual short program to decide which program layout I would skate for that. He very reluctantly agreed with this plan, since he knew I was very set on proving something to myself and that nothing he could say would really dissuade me.

Even my training routine, which should have been consistent, was constantly changing in the weeks before PyeongChang. Generally, I started skating at nine or so in the morning for about three hours, with breaks in between. But I train better in the late afternoon, so I decided to stay for another session at the end of the day, especially if the morning sessions didn't go well. Not surprisingly, that increase in the volume of my training burned me out. But at the time, I thought I was doing what all Olympic hopefuls did. I thought training until you were exhausted was what you needed to do to become an Olympian, not to mention an Olympic champion. I was just trying to mimic what other Olympic skaters had done, hoping for the same results. I had heard that Evan Lysacek did something similar when he was training for the 2010 Vancouver Games. Apparently, after his coach, Frank Carroll, would tell him to go home for the day, Evan would go behind Frank's back and do a few more run-throughs at another rink. That reinforced in my head the idea that if extra practices were what it took to become an Olympic champion, I would pile on additional sessions.

My "Olympic gold or bust" mantra only intensified the closer I got to February. At my last practice in California before leaving for South Korea, Raf asked me if I felt ready. I answered yes, but neither of us were convinced.

The weight of expectations—from myself, my family, and my team—was almost unbearable.

To get to PyeongChang, I flew from Los Angeles to Seoul. Instead of excitment, all I could think about was that I was flying to the biggest event I had ever been to, and how much I needed to accomplish at the Olympics. When I saw all the Olympics rings everywhere just before boarding the flight to South Korea, I remember thinking, "How am I going to make this happen?" Raf, my mom, and Adam Rippon, who also trained with Raf, were on the flight. The whole way over, I was trying to relax, but all I could think about were the expectations of the Olympics—and whether I was going to be able to meet them.

As soon as I landed in Seoul, my anxiety translated into an obsession with the need to start training right away. I was on a mission. We had to go through team processing at a hotel near the airport, which took a while, since all of us had to sign in and get our credentials. In the hotel, there was exercise equipment there for us to use after the long flight, and I made a beeline for the treadmill. My luggage was still on its way, and I didn't have a pair of running shoes on me, so I asked Adam if I could borrow his. I got on a treadmill and started doing sprints, which was not even something that I usually did. A general rule of thumb for athletes at any competition—and especially at the Olympics—is to stick to your normal training routine, a rule I immediately broke as soon I arrived. After we dropped off our stuff at the Village, I asked Brandon if we could find the gym and start my lifting routine. My body was so tired from the travel and from the hard training I had been doing the weeks before I left, but I didn't care.

The Olympics are a whirlwind—there are so many sports going on, so many competitions, so many medals being won, and so many goals being achieved. It's a crazy atmosphere to be in for the athletes. So, U.S. Figure Skating arranged for us to train in Chuncheon, outside Gangneung, where the skating competition was held, so we could practice in a calmer atmosphere and not have to worry about the media and other spectators watching us.

Chuncheon is about an hour's drive from Gangneung. It was the same rink U.S. skaters had used a year earlier for practice, during the Four Continents event, so I had good memories of that ice. My practices before Four Continents at that rink were some of my best; I was landing the quad loop, which I hadn't been landing reliably before; my Lutz was very consistent; and my Salchow and toe were automatic. I was landing a substantial amount of jumps, including the triple Axels, the jump that gives me the most trouble, all in a row. I was hoping for a repeat performance and that being in the same rink would mean I would skate as well as I had then.

But the second time was nothing like the first. This time in Chuncheon, I couldn't land anything.

Once I started practices at the Olympic arena in Gangneung, I remember seeing prominent figure skaters watching our practice—and I remember how awful I felt because I was having trouble with the quad Lutz jump in my short program run-throughs, just as Raf feared I would. I kept significantly underrotating that jump and wasn't even getting close to landing it. And because I had spent so much energy on the Lutz, going into the next two jumps, the quad flip and the triple Axel, I was too tired and made mistakes. That kept happening.

I had been training so hard that my body was unable to rally when I needed it the most. But I didn't understand that then. I couldn't put together any clean run-throughs of my programs. I remember watching the other skaters who were skating so well and checking off clean program after clean program, and thinking, "Why can't I do that?"

My family had rented an Airbnb and everyone was there: my parents; my brothers, Tony and Colin; my sisters, Alice and Janice; Janice's boyfriend (now husband), Orestes; and my uncle's family. I met up with my parents and siblings in the family area in the Athletes' Village and confessed to my mom and my sisters, "I'm so unbelievably nervous." They reassured me that was normal, and just a part of competing; but no matter what they said, my confidence continued to plummet. I felt that I was the only athlete having so much trouble dealing with the pressure of competing at the Olympics. At that point, there wasn't anything anyone could have said to me that would have helped much.

I tried to console myself with the idea that once I got to the venue where the competition would be held, I would skate better. I don't know why I thought that, but I figured that being in the arena would boost my adrenaline and somehow that would get me through the event.

Boy, was I wrong. The day that I was supposed to skate the short program in the team event, I was blindly counting on things to somehow work themselves out and that my jitters were normal precompetition nerves. Just before the skaters got on the ice, we waited in a curtained-off booth until it was our turn to skate out. It's a little Olympic greenroom essentially. I was shaking and sweating—there was a crazy amount of nervous perspiring going on. When my name was called, I got out on the ice and got into position to start my "Nemesis" program. And that's when I looked up and saw those Olympic rings and froze.

I thought, "Why, why did I have to look there?" I tried to avert my eyes, but it was too late—my music had already started. I just couldn't get past those rings and what they meant: I was at the Olympics. I was trying to set up my first jump and my legs didn't cooperate; I felt that I had no strength in my body. I tapped into the quad flip, rushed it, and slipped on my landing so I didn't have enough momentum to do the triple toe I had planned and could only pull off a double toe instead. I then turned my planned quad toe into a double. I heard the audience go "Oooooohhhhh." My next jump was the triple Axel, and I landed too far back and fell. That made it three for three mistakes on my jump passes.

I just wanted to bury myself in the ice and disappear.

I was extremely embarrassed. I didn't want to continue the program—all I could think about in that moment was, "I want to get off the ice."

It was a team event, so after I finally made it through to the end of my program, I had to sit with the rest of Team USA in the box set up by the boards to wait for my scores. It was the last place I wanted to be. I had let them down, and I didn't know what to say to them. Every skater in the team event accumulates points for the team, based on where they finish in the standings; if you finished first, you earned ten points, if you finished second, you earned nine points, and so on. My performance wouldn't be helping Team USA that much.

After the scores came out and I could escape, I immediately ran downstairs to the practice rink underneath the arena. I didn't even take my skates off, or my costume, but tramped to that practice ice to try those jumps again.

Another skater in the men's event was there for his usually scheduled practice, and he was surprised to see me. "Didn't you just compete?" he asked.

"Yeah, I skated like absolute garbage. I didn't do anything," I told him. Then I skated onto the ice with tears welling in my eyes, trying to do these jumps and falling and falling. I had no idea what to do.

As I calmed down, I started to rationalize what had happened. I thought, "Well, at least I got my bad skate out of the way; for the individual short, in the men's event, it will be better." Not that the team event wasn't important, but I was trying to put it behind me as best as I could.

The funny thing is—well, looking back it's funny, but it wasn't at the time—the only way that I knew how to cope with approaching my next event was through superstition. I thought, "If I can tie my skates in a different way, maybe it'll be better." Or "If I shower at a certain time, or plug in my phone in a certain way, things will be better." Anything that deviated from how I had done things before the team short program must lead to a better outcome on the ice. I didn't understand why I wasn't skating well, since I thought I was doing everything I needed to do, eating and preparing properly. Without any answers, I resorted to following this mystique of trying to find some supernatural way to get myself back in the competition again.

But athletics don't work that way.

Part of my spiral had to do with being isolated from my support network. My family was there, but because I was in the Olympic Village, they weren't as accessible to me. And I was so busy with practices, training, and recovery that I couldn't spend that much time with them. I didn't have any other people near me in the Athletes' Village whom I was comfortable talking to. I was also so shy and stressed that I don't think I gave off a very approachable vibe either, which probably isolated me even more. So I spent a lot of time sitting in my room, ruminating and coming up with these outlandish ideas for how I could skate better.

I should have reached out to someone at U.S. Figure Skating for help. But it never dawned on me that I needed mental support—I still thought my issues were all physical. I chalked it up to being super nervous before a competition, especially this competition, the Olympics, and tried to figure out ways to solve my problem physically. It never occurred to me to ask for help—especially from anyone outside of my team. I relied on my mom, and I relied on Raf, and if they didn't say anything that I thought was helpful, or have anything specific to tell me, well, then that was it.

I was on my own.

We had a few days after the team event and before the men's individual short program, so I went back to Chuncheon. My mom and I made the final decision to go back to the quad Lutz–triple toe, along with the quad flip and triple Axel for the short program, because that was the layout I had trained all season until I injured my ankle before Nationals. We rationalized that since I had trained that layout longer, my body was more accustomed to it, while I wasn't used to doing the quad flip–triple toe layout I had tried and failed to pull off in the team event. But Raf continued to be adamant that the latter series was the right choice, since my ankle couldn't handle the Lutz well and I hadn't been able to train the Lutz much in the weeks just before the Olympics. He felt even with the easier jumps, I had a better chance of winning.

But I had faith in my abilities and wanted to give the harder program a try, as my mom suggested. My family attended my practices in Chuncheon and watched me run through my short program and go for a quad Lutz, fall, get up, start my program over, go for the quad Lutz, fall, get up, start my program over. I eventually stopped trying to skate through my program with the music and just tried landing the quad Lutz by itself. And I could barely even do that.

My mom took videos of my falls so I could try and figure out what I was doing wrong, but there was no clear problem. I simply couldn't do the elements. Finally, I thought, "Maybe I have to relax myself mentally." But the more I fell, the more disheartened and frustrated

I became. I had hit a complete mental and physical block. None of the practices I had in that time gave me any confidence. I would always exit the ice less confident than I felt before I got on the ice. Relaxing wasn't an option.

Going into the individual short program, I was hoping the stars would align. I was working myself into exhaustion, and it didn't help that my precompetition warm-up routines made me even more tired. That season, I was in the habit of doing a significant amount of warm-up before every event. I headed to the ice rink about an hour and a half before I was scheduled to skate, and went through an hour-long warm-up routine, which meant I was tired out before I had even tied my skates on.

The warm-up before a competition is a tricky balance. If I don't do anything, I don't feel ready enough or mentally engaged enough to skate well. But looking back, as with everything else that season, I was trying to do too much. Even Brandon agreed that in hindsight, we probably overdid the warm-up. He, like me, was going through trial and error to come up with the best strength and conditioning exercises to prepare me for my challenging programs but still take into account my injuries. But neither of us really knew what it took to get me ready and limber to compete at the level I hoped for. We thought, especially given my hip, that the more I activated my muscles before I got on the ice, the better I would feel. But my warm-up routines had gotten very intensive, far more than they really needed to be.

As soon as I stepped onto the ice for the individual short program, it was the exact same situation as before the team short program a few days before—the exact same feeling. I thought, "Oh no, I don't think I'm capable of doing this." This time, it was almost worse because I couldn't shake the memory of what had happened a few days earlier.

Against Raf's advice, I decided to go for the quad Lutz to open the program, rather than the quad flip. When I fell on that first jump, my first thought was, "I really wish I could go back and restart this program." But of course that wasn't an option. Instead, I allowed myself to get caught up in a complicated game of trying to make up for that initial mistake by mentally mixing and matching the remaining two jumping passes to maximize my points. I had spent so much energy getting up from that fall, I started to think, "How can I adjust my program to potentially get a higher score and conserve my energy so I don't miss every single jump in this program?" I made a last-minute decision to swap out the planned quad flip for the easier quad toe in the second half of the program, but I wasn't mentally prepared for that jump. And while I was busy worrying about that, I did exactly what I feared—I messed up each of my three jump passes. Again.

I stepped out of my quad toe and did the same after landing my triple Axel. I was so off-balance that I had to put my hand down on the ice.

If I had set my mind on one short program—either the one Raf suggested or the one I had wanted to perform—and stuck to it no matter what happened, I probably would have been able to salvage both those disastrous short programs, or at least scrape together something that would have been better than what I actually performed. Having too many backup options, and too many combinations running through my head, when I should have been focused on following through on what I had practiced all season, introduced too much room for error and ended up setting me up for failure.

Coming off the ice, I couldn't look at Raf or anyone else in the arena. I knew I would just see disappointment. I hadn't received scores that low in years. I wanted to slink away from the bright lights of the arena.

I didn't want to talk to the media, I wanted to get out of the rink as quickly as I could. I didn't know that I was allowed to skip the mixed zone, which is this gauntlet of reporters who pepper you with a bunch of questions. So I faced them. I remember the reporters were really gentle, maybe because they were as shocked as I was and didn't know what to make of what had happened. They asked me, "How do you feel?"

I answered, "I don't feel good," and that was pretty much it.

By the time everyone had skated, I was in seventeenth place out of two dozen skaters. As soon as my press obligations were done, I slipped out of the arena and went back to my room in the Village. I just wanted to lie in bed and not think at all.

I can't remember if I called my mom, or if she called me as she was walking out of the arena with my family, but we talked.

"Do me a favor, Nathan," she said.

"What?" I responded.

"Just skate a clean long tomorrow. You can do it."

I desperately wanted to do the same, but wasn't in any mindset to make promises. It was my mom's way of encouraging me. Her philosophy in parenting all her children was to never give up. She wanted us to work hard and train hard for the best results; but if things didn't go well, she also wanted us to push on despite the result. That's why she had told Genia that I would still skate at the novice championships so many years ago, even though I had been injured three weeks before the competition. Even if I came in last, if I didn't even try, then I would never know what I could accomplish. Her one sentence request embodied all that: by asking me to skate a clean free program, she was telling me that the competition wasn't over yet.

At the time, though, I didn't want to think about what had happened at all. For the next eighteen hours I just lay in bed under my blankets. It was still relatively early in the afternoon, since the competition had been in the morning, but I closed the shades and didn't eat anything. I just lay there in the darkness. At some point, I got up to take a shower and then tried to go to sleep. But sleep had eluded me ever since I arrived in PyeongChang. I was only half sleeping, which meant I never felt fully physically recovered. I was used to sleeping close to ten hours at home, but was not getting nearly that over the past few days. Since I was struggling with it now, I started to panic.

I kept tossing and turning, until finally, I called Alice.

"I can't sleep. What should I do?" I asked. "Should I take Tylenol PM?"

I had brought some Tylenol PM to PyeongChang just in case I needed it to help me fall asleep. I had previously used it, but I would feel drowsy and not as responsive the next morning. I had an early morning practice for the free program the next day, and I didn't want to feel drowsy on the ice.

Alice was at the Airbnb and decided to consult with the whole family. We figured it was okay for me to take one so I could sleep and still get up relatively early the next morning. I didn't really want to get into a discussion about anything else at that point, and I think my family sensed that and respected it. As soon as we decided I could take a Tylenol PM, I hung up.

That night I got the best night's sleep during the whole time I was in South Korea. I woke up the next morning well rested and was feeling really fresh for the free program, which was scheduled at 10 A.M. The further back in the standings you are, the earlier your practice time, so I was among the first skaters at the rink that morning.

In the back of my mind, I was wondering if there was any point in trying six quads, as Raf and I had planned, since my practices had been so inconsistent. I had made every mistake possible on my jumps in the two short programs I had skated so far, so I figured, what difference would it make if I made a few more? I was beyond worrying about the outcome at that point. I had nothing to lose: falling further back in the placements wouldn't change anything, and winning a medal was off the table. My mom and Tony were at my practice that morning; and though we didn't talk, I did make eye contact with my mom, which made me feel a little better. I knew she was rooting for me no matter what had happened. Tony was being very supportive—and loud. There weren't many people in the rink at that hour, so I could hear him screaming "Go, Nathan!" or "Yeah, Nathan" every time I landed a jump. With all the pressure finally dissipated, I skated a clean run-through of my program during that practice.

During that session, Yuzuru came in for his practice session. I was still on the ice as he was just arriving and started to warm up. He was, of course, in the lead after the short program, with a 4.1 point margin over Javier Fernandez, who was in second. Maybe I was projecting how I was feeling, but to me, it looked like Yuzuru was taking in the moment and really savoring being at his second Olympics and perhaps on the verge of defending his Olympic title. That's not an easy place to be, and he also had a lot of pressure on him to repeat as Olympic champion, which hadn't been done since Dick Button in 1948 and 1952. But rather than looking anxious or uncomfortable with all those expectations, he seemed calm and just grateful for the chance to be there competing. I remember realizing that I hadn't experienced those feelings once during this competition. I didn't talk to him, or ask him how he was feeling; and maybe it was just in my own mind, because my Olympics had been so stress filled and disappointing, but it's something that stood out for me from that practice.

My mentality going into the free program was entirely different from what it was before the short program. I didn't care about the results anymore. It's not that I wasn't thankful for the opportunity to skate at the Olympics, something that I had dreamed so long of doing, but my goal had drastically changed. I talked briefly to my family, and through texts, they were telling me to focus on that gratitude—as poorly as my two previous programs had gone, I still had another opportunity to compete. And that was more than many athletes could hope for.

At that point, it was no longer about where I placed. I wasn't focused on getting the highest levels for my spins or my footwork, and I didn't really care if I fell on every single jump. I told myself my goal was to start the program when the music began and end it when the music finished, and whatever happened in between would happen.

As unappreciative as that approach seems, that mentality was what I needed to counter the "Olympic gold or bust" thinking that had weighed me down to that point. Sitting in seventeenth place, I had almost nowhere to go but up, so that might have freed me to finally skate at the level I knew I was capable of reaching. And somehow, I did. I stayed upright on all six quad jumps, and won the free skate portion of the event.

I had done what my mom had asked me to do.

Even though I won the free skate, there was practically no chance of earning a medal; the short and free program scores are combined, and my short program's score pulled me quite far down in the rankings. Still, a tiny flame of hope ignited after I finished my free skate. I thought to myself, "You never know what happens in figure skating. If all the top seven guys make mistakes on almost all their jumps—and that's a possibility, although a very small one—I could sneak onto the podium." It was very unlikely, but I sat patiently and watched competitor after competitor take the ice. But as each skater in the last group competed, I saw my name drop further and further back.

Still, I was proud of myself for getting through the program and happy for all the athletes who got to experience their Olympic moment. But I was ready to put the entire Games behind me, and start looking ahead to the World Championships, which were a month later.

5 NEW CHALLENGES

世上无难事, 只怕有心人

Nothing is impossible if you put your mind into it.

A couple of days after I finished competing, I got sick. I felt achy and had a fever, so I went to the sports medicine clinic in the Olympic Athletes' Village. They did a rapid flu test and I tested positive. To protect the other athletes who were still competing, they moved me to housing outside the Olympic Village. I had been invited to skate at the exhibition, but since I was sick, I couldn't attend any practice sessions and I didn't think I would be ready. Since my family had the Airbnb in Seoul, I decided to finish my quarantine and leave the Olympics early to stay with them.

With my entire family there, it turned out to be a nice reunion and mini vacation. I thought the mood would be off and that everyone would be ruminating about how I had skated—after all, the Games hadn't exactly turned out the way any of us expected. Instead, they told me they were proud of me after my free skate; before the music even ended, my entire family—including my uncle, aunt, and cousins—and my agent, Yuki Saegusa—were all jumping out of their seats, shouting my name and crying. My mom told me how proud she was and thought all my hard work really showed in that program. We found some great restaurants, enjoyed Korean BBQ, and toured Seoul. It had been a long time since all of us were together, and it helped to take my mind off skating for a little bit. I didn't skate during that time, although I kind of watched the women's competition a few days after I finished competing—out of the corner of my eye while it was on TV.

I knew for sure I wanted to compete at the World Championships, which were in Milan, Italy, in March, and I for sure wanted to have another shot at competing my two programs—especially the short program. With the Games behind me, it became almost like a challenge—I wanted to prove to myself that I could do it. I was also humbled by the incredible amount of support I received from my fans and other athletes, and buoyed by their faith in me. Serena Williams even DM'd me and graciously invited me to reach out to her for advice or anything else I needed. That meant a lot to me, and I am so grateful for her generosity as a fellow athlete; especially since we hadn't met.

The free program in PyeongChang definitely boosted my confidence a bit, so I went back home to California feeling better and ready to work. I focused on getting back into shape after taking a few days off in South Korea. I decided I would skate the short program layout Raf and I had trained for most of the season, before I injured my ankle, with the quad Lutz–triple toe, the quad flip, and the triple Axel. And for the free program, I would keep the six quads I had done at the Olympics.

This was only my second World Championships, but I recall stepping onto the practice ice with a completely new sense of confidence. Maybe my jumps weren't perfectly consistent, but I had the sensation of being in sync with my body and feeling everything was falling into place. Maybe it was the switch in mentality. Again, as I had before the free program in PyeongChang, in Milan, I thought, "I'm not going to worry about the elements, I'll just go for it."

I skated pretty well in the short program and landed all my jumps, despite being a bit shaky on some of the landings. I was really happy with the way I skated. In my free program, just like at the Olympics, I stood up on all six quads. So I counted that as a win. I won my first World Championship title, and it was a good confidence builder.

As soon as I finished my free program in PyeongChang, I knew that I wanted to train for another Olympic cycle. There wasn't a question in my mind that I wanted another chance to compete at the Olympic Games, not necessarily to win but to skate in a way that would make me feel fulfilled and satisfied that I had done my best.

I wasn't quite sure what those next four years would entail, but as it happened, I got another life-changing opportunity. And oddly enough, it came from outside the skating world.

Soon after I finished competing at the World Championships in Italy, I left to skate in Japan on the Stars on Ice tour. While I was there, I received the exciting news that I had been accepted to Yale! Since education has always been important in my family, I always knew I wanted to follow my brothers and sisters to college. I was also eager to start exploring a world outside of figure skating, and felt my best path toward that was through college. I had applied to colleges in December 2017, but because I was so focused on Nationals and the Olympics, I wasn't thinking about it too much until I heard back. I was so excited, I called my mom immediately. She was happy for me, but of course started thinking about how to make my skating training fit in with a college course load. Having that acceptance was hugely reassuring, and being able to count that as another win made me feel like I was back on the right track.

I also knew that if training for 2018 had been challenging, the next four years would prove even more difficult if I had to juggle classes with a full skating schedule. In addition, the men's skating field was changing, and the cast of skaters would be quite different in 2022. Some of the top male skaters I had been competing against, like world champions Javier Fernandez and Patrick Chan, were retiring, and that would reshape the field considerably. I was keeping an eye on the junior skaters, too, and seeing who was coming up. A few of the junior skaters, and some of the senior-level competitors who would continue for another Olympic cycle, were performing technical content at a level similar to that of the top skaters in PyeongChang. So for the next few years, I knew that if I maintained the level I had reached, I could stay competitive. And I couldn't wait for the chance to compete at another Games, now that I had experienced competing at one. I knew what to expect at the Games and felt better equipped to navigate the next Olympics.

I just had to figure out how to do that while going to school.

Raf was thrilled with the news about Yale and very supportive about my decision to attend college. He said he would miss training with me and made it clear that he wanted me back to train, preferably after two years, to prepare for the 2022 Winter Olympics. He knew I was capable of maintaining the work we had started over the next two years and didn't think it was crucial for me to be in California during that time. But beginning in 2020, he wanted me to start focusing more seriously on 2022. Both he and Brandon felt confident that even though I would be across the country in New Haven, Connecticut, we could work out periodic check-ins and keep my training on track. My mom, however, was a bit more concerned about my keeping up a training schedule, and she wanted to know exactly how I would be able to maintain the same number of hours on the ice.

My agent, Yuki; my mom; and I visited Yale during Bulldog Days, a kind of orientation event for admitted students and their families to get familiar with the school. I talked to my advisers there. It turned out that my classes could be scheduled mostly in the mornings, so my afternoons would be free for skating. That was close enough to how I had generally scheduled my days up to that point, so we all were feeling very comfortable with the idea that going to college and continuing to skate would work out. I was going to have a bit less ice time than I was used to, but we were confident that it was going to be enough to get me through the next year or so.

I started thinking about creating my skating programs for the next season, as I always do in the summer, and decided to work with Shae-Lynn Bourne again. She had choreographed my short program for the 2018 Olympics, to Benjamin Clementine's "Nemesis," and I loved working with her. She was an ice dancer who skated for Canada with Victor Kraatz in the late 1990s and early 2000s. In 2003, they were the first ice dance team from North America to win a World Championship, breaking the decades-long string of eastern European winners. She and Victor competed at three Olympics, finishing fourth in 1998 in Nagano, Japan, and fourth again in 2002 in Salt Lake City, when I was just starting to skate. As a choreographer, she worked with top skaters from around the world; she created Yuzuru's 2018 Olympic winning free program.

Shae was based in Charleston, South Carolina, at the time, so I flew there over the summer and spent about a week putting together a program set to "Caravan," a Duke Ellington piece that's full of energy and flair—very different from the moodier "Nemesis."

Shae is an amazing and incredibly creative choreographer with a sixth sense for the type of music that suits each skater. She keeps a list of potential pieces for each skater she works with and has phenomenal instincts for interpreting music. The upbeat vibe of "Caravan" felt like the right music for the next season, after the more somber pieces I'd used in 2018.

Once Shae and I had worked out the basics for my short program, I turned my attention to the free program. From the start of that summer, I had thought that having a different choreographer for my free would be a good change, and I was eager to explore someone new. I had worked with Shae, Lori Nichol, Nikolai Morozov, Nadia Kanaeva, and

Marina Zoueva. Lori Nichol collaborated with some champion skaters and created memorable programs, including Michelle Kwan's Salome program in 1996 and Evan Lysacek's Olympic gold-medal winning programs. Lori is very, very experienced and has a great vision for putting together an Olympic-worthy program—she had created my 2018 Olympic free program. I thought it was a good time to experiment with different pieces of music and different choreographers, and was learning that I enjoyed skating to music that is more contemporary. That prompted me to think about Marie-France Dubreuil.

At the 2018 Games, I had watched the ice dancers from the Ice Academy of Montreal (I.AM) compete and train at the practice rinks and was really impressed with how fresh and innovative their programs were. Marie and her husband, Patrice Lauzon, who competed in ice dance for Canada at the Olympics twice and won two World silver medals, were their coaches and choreographers. Their movements were so cool and precise, and their programs carried a distinctive signature. I knew Marie did most of the choreography, and I thought working with her would give my free program a different feel and add new depth to my skating.

Raf agreed, and suggested that I reach out, so I got her number and sent her a text. Marie and I went back and forth. At first she wasn't sure about the idea. She told me she hadn't worked much with singles skaters, so wasn't as familiar with the rules for singles skating and didn't want to provide choreographic content that wouldn't suit or help me. She was used to working with two people, and finding ways to meld their movements. As a singles skater, I was only half the package. She instead recommended that I contact a friend of hers who had more experience designing a program for a singles skater. I wasn't deterred and remained persistent. I told her that if she was worried about choreographing jump setups, that wouldn't be an issue—Raf and I had already worked out a number of different layouts, as we al-

Still in diapers, soon after we moved into our house in Salt Lake City. Alice is clearly enjoying watching me perform one of the dance routines she was trying to teach me.

Me and my brothers, Tony and Colin, in front of Rice-Eccles Stadium at the University of Utah, where the Olympic cauldron burned during the Winter Olympics in Salt Lake City, 2002. As I look back, this is probably where my Olympic journey really began.

The Chen kids at Yellowstone National Park in 2001—Tony, me, Alice, Colin, and Janice.

Alice took this photo of Janice, in pink, me (in my first, white skates), Colin, and Tony at Steiner, having fun on the ice.

Unless otherwise noted, all photos © Nathan Chen.

When I was young, my family traveled almost every weekend to attend a chess tournament, since all my siblings played. Many of these tournaments were in Las Vegas, and this photo was taken there in 2002 during one of them—with Alice, Tony, me, Janice, and Colin.

Stephanee Grosscup, my first skating coach, and me in 2003 at the Utah Winter Games, my very first skating competition.

My dad, me, and my mom at the Utah Winter Games in 2003. That was the first of many costumes my mom made for my skating programs.

Karel Kovar, the coach who laid the foundation for my jumping technique, and me at some point in 2005–2006. My mom would drive me from Salt Lake City to Ogden, Utah, for lessons with Karel.

Me at a piano recital in Salt Lake City in 2005. I had come a long way from banging on the toy piano I picked out at Toys 'R Us.

Me, Stephanee Grosscup, and Genia Chernyshova in Jackson Hole, Wyoming, for a competition in 2009. Stephanee and Genia taught me strong skating fundamentals that have made me the skater I am today.

Me competing at the 2010 Utah State Gymnastics championships, on parallel bars. I started gymnastics because my mom felt it would help to build the strength I needed to become a strong figure skater.

Me on the sign for Ice Castle in 2011, soon after I started training there with Rafael.

My sister Janice and me at the U.S. Olympic and Paralympic Committee facility in Chula Vista, California, in 2016, two weeks after my hip surgery. I wasn't supposed to put any weight my left leg, so Janice is mimicking by standing on one leg.

My mom, me, Janice, and Orestes, in Sun Valley, Idaho, in summer 2014, where I skated in the Sun Valley ice show.

Dick Button, Raf, and me in January 2018. It was an honor to meet Dick and he wished me luck in my skating career. *(Credit: Barb Reichert/U.S. Figure Skating)*

The 2018 Olympic U.S. figure skating team, dressed for Opening Ceremonies. This was the first and only Opening Ceremonies I attended (I didn't march in 2022 because I had to compete a few days later and I didn't want to risk getting COVID-19). I'm third from left in the front row.

Tina Lundgren, ice dancer Madison Chock, and me before Opening Ceremonies in 2018. Tina, a world figure skating judge and member of the U.S. Figure Skating Board of Directors, has been so supportive throughout my skating career, and has given me valuable feedback on my programs. She helped me to consider bringing back *Rocketman* for my 2022 Olympic free program.

My family—Colin, Alice, me, Tony, Mom, Janice, Dad—came to the press center after Team USA won the bronze in the team event at the 2018 Olympics in PyeongChang, Korea. It was my first Olympic medal, and everyone was so happy for me.

My entire family came to support me at the PyeongChang Olympics in 2018, and they were really excited after my free skate. *From left, behind the top flag:* Orestes, Janice, Tony. *Middle row:* Colin, Alice, my cousins Kevin and Jerome, my aunt Xiaohua, and uncle Jing. *Bottom row:* my dad, my mom, and Yuki. *(Credit: Chris Detrick—the Salt Lake Tribune)*

First day as a college student! This was moving day, in August 2018, in front of my dorm with my mom.

Me chilling in my first year dorm at Yale University in New Haven, Connecticut. I'm using compression pants that help my muscles to recover more quickly by enhancing blood circulation.

Mary Liu, professor of history and American studies at Yale, Michelle Kwan, me, and Vicky Chun, director of athletics at Yale, in April 2019 in New Haven after Michelle gave a talk at the college. Michelle has been, and continues to be, a huge inspiration and role model to me as a Chinese American.

Shae-Lynn Bourne and me in Charleston, South Carolina, during one of our choreography sessions.

Sam Chouinard, Marie-France Dubreuil, and me at Ice Academy of Montreal in 2019. We were making final tweaks to the *Rocketman* program they had choreographed for me before the Grand Prix Final later that month. We didn't know then that I would end up using that program again for the Olympics in 2022.

Me and Colin playing chess at my sister's house in May 2021. Everyone in my family are skilled players; I'm probably the least proficient but am trying to catch up. I started playing with my mom just for fun in the season leading up to Beijing.

My 2022 Olympic skating boot, with an impromptu leather addition in the front of the tongue by Raf. The added piece gave me the additional stiffness I needed to land my jumps when my boots started to break down too quickly.

I had fun shooting several commercials before the Beijing Olympics with my various sponsors. On one shoot, I was able to get some playing time in on a guitar.

Janice took this picture of my family at her house in San Francisco as they watched me skate in the individual short program in Beijing in 2022. *From left:* my dad, Colin, my mom, and Orestes. You can't see Alice and other family members who were linked in on Zoom.

This was right after my free skate at the 2022 Olympics in Beijing. I've worked with Brandon Siakel, my strength and conditioning coach, since 2015, and he has helped me through injuries, surgery, rehab, and two Olympics. He gave me a big hug and told me he was proud of me.

Raf holding the gold that both he and I worked so hard for.

Raf, me, and Brandon at a practice session for the exhibition after the competitions were over in Beijing.

Me in front of the Bird's Nest Stadium in Beijing at the Olympics in 2022, after the men's competition, with Mitch Moyer.

Tina Lundgren wanted to see my gold medal, so I brought it, box and all, to an exhibition practice.

I did two of these obligatory photo shoots on the Olympic rings in the Olympic Village in February 2022, one right at the beginning of the Games, and another, when this was taken, toward the end.

Jean-Luc Baker, one of the Team USA ice dancers, and me before Closing Ceremonies in Beijing in February 2022. Jean-Luc was one of my first roommates when I started traveling for skating competitions as a junior skater, and we've been friends ever since.

The boys of Suite 502—Brandon Frazier, me, Jean-Luc Baker, and Evan Bates—ready for Closing Ceremonies at the 2022 Olympics in Beijing.

The entire U.S. Olympic figure skating team, including some of the officials and medical staff who supported us, before we marched in Closing Ceremonies in Beijing in February 2022.

I flew straight from the Beijing Games to New York City for an appearance on the *Today* show on February 22. I appreciated all the people who showed up so early in the morning at Rockefeller Center with signs to cheer me on.

My mom surprised me on the *Today* show in New York City. When I first saw her, I thought she was some weird doppelgänger because I wasn't expecting to see her there. As soon as I realized it was really her, I gave her a big hug and thanked her. *(Credit: NBC's TODAY)*

My first thought after seeing my mom was to give her my medal, which I did, and she was surprised by how heavy it was. *(Credit: NBC's TODAY)*

n the green room with Alice and Jimmy allon. He was really nice and one of the indest famous people I've met.

Chilling in the classroom of Professor Jing Tsu, Professor of East Asian Languages and Literatures & Comparative Literature Chair, in April 2022 at Yale before speaking on a panel about my perspective as an Asian American athlete.

Me with my first and only agent, Yuki Saegusa from IMG, in New York in June 2022. Yuki has supported me and my family throughout the ups and downs of my skating career.

The sketch that Vera Wang made for my free program costume for the *Rocketman* program, which I ended up wearing at the Beijing Olympics. This costume is a part of the permanent collections in the Smithsonian Institution's National Museum of American History.

This was another design for the *Rocketman* program, with a pop of color that Vera added to make it stand out. I wore this one at the 2022 U.S. National Championships, before the Beijing Olympics.

ways do, and she could just build from that. Plus, I'd be going to school on the East Coast; New Haven was only an hour and a half flight from Montreal, so I wouldn't be dropping in once and disappearing, but ready for an ongoing dialogue to create the right program. That seemed to make her more comfortable, and she finally agreed.

I went to Montreal that summer and spent a week working with Marie and Patch (which is what all the ice dancers call Patrice) and soaking in the great training atmosphere at I.AM. I had become good friends with one of the ice dancers she coached, Jean-Luc Baker. Jean-Luc, who had been training in Michigan, had moved to Montreal with his partner, Kaitlin Hawayek, to work with Marie and Patch that spring, so I stayed with him for a week. Jean-Luc was one of my first roommates when I was competing in juniors, and we hit it off right away and became great friends. He had told me a lot about the training atmosphere at I.AM. The more I heard, the more I wanted to see it for myself.

It didn't disappoint. I've always loved training with ice dancers. I really enjoyed the time I spent with them and Marina Zoueva in Michigan in 2016, and it was the same in Montreal. Spending time in the invigorating atmosphere that Marie and Patch had created was exactly what I needed after my challenging Olympic year. I find dance environments are always so positive and friendly, and I was fascinated by the way Marie and Patch structured their training sessions. They have about two dozen top teams from all over the world training there, including Gabriella Papadakis and Guillaume Cizeron from France, who won silver in 2018 and became Olympic champions in 2022; Madison Hubbell and Zachary Donohue from the United States, who would win bronze in Beijing; Madison Chock and Evan Bates from the United States, who were three-time World medalists; and several of the top teams from other countries. At the Beijing Olympics, Marie and Patch and their team were coaching eleven of the twenty-three dance teams competing.

Being in Montreal reinvigorated my love for skating and reminded me of how exciting competing could be. I do love jumping and especially the challenge of breaking down the mechanics of the rotation, torque, and angles involved. But if you just do jump training repetitively for a really long time, it can become monotonous. Training in Montreal broke that routine for me. With the ice dancers, there was always something I'd never seen before, whether it was the patterns that they were carving on the ice or the choreography that they were developing in collaboration with their coaches. The only other time I had been around ice dancers was when I was training with Marina Zoueva in Michigan. I loved it then, but now that I was older, I appreciated training with the teams at I.AM even more. It brought the artistic side of my skating to a deeper level that I hoped would set my programs apart. It was clear how much the dancers cherished and enjoyed skating, bringing drama and characters to the ice. Ice dancers have to rely on a multitude of details to appeal to the judges and the audience—through every edge their skate blades make on the ice and every arm, head, and body movement in their choreography. Creating a program that isn't built around jumps takes an extraordinary amount of time and effort, and it was fascinating to witness how the process worked.

Watching firsthand how Marie and Patch managed their time with their skaters was also helpful, as I was just at the beginning stages of thinking about how to adjust my own training regimen once I started school. It was really useful to see how efficient they were with every minute they were on the ice. My productivity during training had a lot of room for growth, because I was often not focusing on the right thing or because I was trying to battle through frustration and getting stuck in a cycle of bad habits. Seeing how the dancers deliberately planned every minute of their time on the ice and what they would work on helped me appreciate the importance of quality over quantity. That understanding was key to eventually coming up with my own training schedule that balanced skating with my academic responsibilities.

That summer, the first program I worked on with Marie was called "Land of All." I had already decided I wanted to skate to music from Woodkid, a French music video director and singer-songwriter. I had been listening to his music for a while but I didn't know if Marie would think it was right for a skating program. Yet when I played it for her, she also saw its potential and even suggested adding a cello introduction to start it off. We dove right in and within a few days, finished the program. I was actually a little surprised by how chill and relaxed she was. I knew she was working with some of the best ice dancers in the world, and I had this preconceived notion that maybe she was going to be uptight and very strict and specific about what she wanted—especially since in ice dancing everything has to be so precise and clean. But instead, she was very low-key and really fun to work with. Everything felt so open and creative; choreographing that program was really a collaborative effort. She would give me ideas for movements, ask me to try them, and if they didn't feel right, I'd propose a variation and we'd go from there. She made me feel comfortable in taking some authority and letting her know which movements I liked and which movements didn't feel right.

I also had the chance to work with one of her choreographers, Samuel Chouinard, whom Marie and Patch hired to give their ice dancers more dance training. Sam is an amazing hip-hop dancer and a ball of energy—he's always so positive and creative. Before coming to I.AM, he didn't know how to skate and had never really worked with skaters, but after contributing to a few programs for Joannie Rochette, the Canadian Olympic bronze medalist from the 2010 Games, he caught the eye of Marie and Patch. Sam learned to skate and gets on the ice with whomever he is working with, and has mastered how to transfer dance moves to the ice. Working with him was like working with a dancer, not a figure skating coach. He brings a perspective to movements that was unlike any other that I was used to. He left a signature mark on my program and unlocked a new, more confident persona for me on the ice—the fun footwork sequences and the high energy in my programs are all thanks to Sam.

Sam and I would start working in the studio with some moves, and then we'd switch to the ice and work with Marie. That season, I wanted to scale back on my quads a little, while still keeping myself competitive. We designed that free program with three quads, but I always had the option to add another if I felt I needed to. Every time I made a judgment call to add an extra quad that season it was dependent on whom I was competing against. I remember at one of the Grand Prix events, I knew Shoma Uno from Japan would be competing. I added another quad, just to make sure I had enough points to keep up with him, since I knew he was a strong technical and artistic skater.

Still, that season, the first one during which I competed while I was in college, I decided to be realistic about how much training I could get and what I could handle. Rather than going for the hardest jump layouts, I recognized that it was more important to be able to train a program I could execute consistently in practice than to attempt to compete the hardest program that I could do.

Managing a full course load as a first-year at Yale while maintaining my skating training forced me to make some changes in the way I practiced.

I was very lucky; everyone on my team, as well as Mitch Moyer at U.S. Figure Skating, really went out of their way to make sure I had everything I needed to make the most of being a college student while continuing to train for the Olympics.

By the time I started classes in the fall of 2018, I felt pretty comfortable with my new setup. Mitch, Yuki, and Brandon had already visited Yale and talked to the folks in the athletic department to work out ice time for me at the Whale, Yale's skating facility, as well as time at the gym for my strength and conditioning exercises.

The Whale is technically named the David S. Ingalls Rink, after a former Yale ice hockey captain, but it's called the Whale because the curved roof and rising tail resemble the back of a humpback whale. It's an amazing feat of architecture designed by Eero Saarinen, a Yale architecture alum from the 1930s who also designed the St. Louis Gateway Arch and the TWA terminal at New York's John F. Kennedy International Airport, both really iconic and amazing pieces of work. The Yale Whale, built in 1959, is signature Saarinen—with ribbed timber beams that feed into a curving concrete spine. When I stepped inside, I almost felt like I was actually in the belly of a whale. It was breathtaking, and I was really honored to have the opportunity to skate there. Seeing the Yale "Y" everywhere was also really cool. Most rinks look the same, and feel pretty sterile. But skating at the Whale was special—the stadium seating made skating there not feel like practice, but like I was skating at a major competition venue.

I was lucky enough to get an hour and a half of ice time a day there, but wanted to stick to my normal schedule of skating three hours a day. So while we were in New Haven that spring, we also scouted Champions Skating Center, about half an hour away. I would be in class in the morning and then after class I would skate on campus, and then immediately drive over to Champions for the afternoon sessions. Fortunately, the former Ingalls Rink Operations lead assistant, George Arnaoutis, went above and beyond trying to help me, and whenever extra ice was available he would try to slot me in for that time. Everything fell into place for me to balance school and skating. Thanks to the support of so many people at Yale and Champions, it felt easy. I arrived at school in good spirits and optimistic that everything would work out.

And for the most part, it did. I was pretty excited to get settled in and find my routine. I was in a suite with five other students, and our suite was connected to another, larger one. As for classes, I didn't know which major I would pick yet, but I was leaning toward doing premed. I figured I should get a science credit out of the way, but I wasn't super concerned about meeting all the prerequisites; I knew I could always do a postbaccalaureate and finish them later before applying to medical school, if that's what I ended up deciding. The obstacle I had with pre-med science classes is that they require a lab that takes several hours one day of the week, from 1 P.M. to 5 P.M., and that's when I needed to train. Fortunately, one of the first required pre-med classes, general chemistry, didn't require taking the lab simultaneously, and I could pick it up later. I ended up also taking calculus, a writing class, and Spanish.

As my classes got busier, I quickly found out I didn't know how to study very efficiently. Everything I'd done for the past few years in high school had been online; and while that had prepared me to be resourceful and independent, the rigor of in-person college classes was more than I had anticipated.

Of course, there are teaching assistants and the professors had office hours, and both were supposed to help us if we ran into problems. But just as I had with my skating, at first I tried to push through on my own. I'm often too shy to approach people for help. I also felt outmatched academically and believed that everyone else knew how to do the assignments on their own, so I should be able to figure it out as well. But I didn't understand that in those first few months that wasn't realistic and I should have taken advantage of the resources that were there to help me.

I spent a good portion of my first semester struggling to stay afloat, especially juggling my competitions. The fall season is the busiest in skating—the Grand Prix series rolls out beginning in October with a competition in a different overseas country every week or so, ending with the Grand Prix Final, which is usually in December. Fortunately, as the world champion I had the opportunity to name which Grand Prix events I wanted to compete at, and had a good chance of being assigned to the events I requested. I chose competitions that would be held during breaks at Yale, but I still missed a few classes, so I started falling behind.

During that fall semester, I had problem sets due every Wednesday afternoon, and that was right during my freestyle skating session at Champions Skating Center. On my busiest weeks, I would sit in the car trying to finish them off, or I'd sit in the lobby of the rink to complete the assignment and submit it before it was due. Those problem sets would take so much time and would sometimes cut into my training time. Which was bad for both skating and school. I was rushing to get the problems done without having the time to understand the concepts well and learn from them. I had to learn how to budget my time better.

Skating-wise, though, overall I had a pretty good season competing in the Grand Prix series, Grand Prix Final, Nationals, and Worlds, with my "Caravan" short program and "Land of All" free program. However, it didn't start out great with my first skate at the Japan Open in early October, a team-based event in which invited skaters compete just their free programs. I liked starting the season with that event because it's lower stakes and a great opportunity to get warmed up for the upcoming competitions. I really didn't feel prepared in the weeks leading up to it, though. I didn't know if I should compete, but I really wanted the chance to skate my programs, so I decided to go. I called my mom and asked her to come out to New Haven and help me train and guide me through my run-throughs, just for a few days, before I had to leave for Japan. I was working on my own at the rink, and didn't have anyone giving me feedback, so I really needed her to provide some insight to my training, which is what she's always done and does really well. I was talking to Raf, but only about once a month or so; we discussed my jump layouts and he basically trusted me to do what I needed to do to get ready for my competitions.

I didn't have the start I wanted at Japan Open and finished fourth, after losing four points for falls. I never like to skate badly, of course, but I reminded myself that, given that it was my first season juggling both skating and school, I shouldn't expect the same results as I had in previous years. I told myself not to dwell on it but to keep improving with each competition.

My first competition in the Grand Prix series that year was Skate America, in Everett, Washington, from October 19 to 21. I went in with a mindset to place high enough to qualify for the Grand Prix Final but prepared myself to not be too disappointed if I didn't skate as well as I wanted. Raf called it "surviving," since our goal was to maintain my technical ability while not worrying about pushing to achieve anything new.

My performances were a little rocky—I stepped out of my quad flip in the short program and landed a little wildly on the quad Lutz in the free, but overall I wasn't particularly stressed. Raf and I had been realistic in designing the free program, and we didn't plan on including four quads in that program from the start. I knew there was no way I could handle that many quads if I wasn't training exclusively, so we toned it down a bit and started with three quads. This plan worked in Everett, and the mindset of building from competition to competition was something I would carry with me over the next four years. While my skate wasn't perfect, it was a big step up from Japan Open, and I won my first competition as a college student.

My next competition was the Internationaux de France during Thanksgiving recess, a month later, in Grenoble, France. Because I had a few days off from school, I flew to Europe early to work on my jumps with Raf in Moscow, where he was at another Grand Prix event. At the CSKA Ice Palace in Moscow, I met the legendary figure skating coach Tatiana Tarasova. The change in training environment and break from classes really amped and energized me while I was training in Moscow, so I went through way more run-throughs of my programs than I would normally have done at Yale. By the time I got to France, I was exhausted. But again, I set my expectations a little lower and tried not to worry too much about the results. Figuring out how to be more realistic helped me to get through that season and the next—and to skate well. Even though I wasn't so focused on skating and winning over the next two years, I managed to win all my competitions.

But it wasn't easy, especially that first semester. During the Grand Prix Final in Vancouver in early December 2018, I remember lying in my bed, stressed because I felt I couldn't manage everything. My skating was going all right; I had faith that I could still be competitive. But school was overwhelming. I had so many deadlines to meet and exams to take, and I never felt I had enough time to prepare. I wasn't even taking super hard classes, so I worried about how well I could manage whatever was in store for me academically in the future.

By the second semester I got a little better at balancing my schoolwork and skating. Through trial and error and necessity, I was slowly beginning to find ways to build the right system for managing my hectic schedule.

In a way, having school become my priority over skating was a relief. I knew I had only a limited amount of mental energy, so I was learning to shift that drive a little more toward school.

During that second semester, I felt more on top of things and less like I was always behind. The skating schedule was a little lighter, and that helped—Nationals are always in January, which is at the beginning of the Yale semester, before we got too deep into a lot of material, and the World Championships were during spring break in March, so I didn't miss any classes.

I had decided to follow a statistics focus, and took more classes that would help me with that, including the next level calculus, linear algebra, coding, and probability classes. I found that I really liked linear algebra—it was fun and I found the content interesting.

Having to prioritize school also served as a reality check for my "go big or go home" mindset. It reinforced the idea that I didn't necessarily have to go for the hardest, most complicated dream program to win but instead had to look realistically at the percentage of successful jumps I landed and come up with the strongest layout that I could perform reliably. And that had to do with taking a hard look at what I was actually accomplishing in practice and sticking with that.

The reality check ended up serving me well. I managed to win my second World title in Saitama that season, and felt like I was finding my footing when it came to my skating. That made three National Championship and two World titles and I had remained undefeated since the 2018 Olympics.

The summer of 2019, before my sophomore year at Yale, Raf moved rinks again, this time to Great Park Ice & FivePoint Arena in Irvine. It's a huge complex, the largest in California and one of the largest ice facilities in the United States. Great Park has three NHL rinks and one Olympic-size rink for figure skating, as well as a twenty-five-hundred-seat arena for shows and hockey games. That summer, as I started to make plans for the upcoming season, I decided that I liked the dichotomy of the two very distinct programs from the previous season, and the mix of working with both Shae and Marie. So, I followed the same strategy and asked Shae to choreograph my short program again and Marie to create my free program.

This time, we switched up the pace of the music in each. "Caravan" was fast paced, joyous, and a little cheeky, so Shae and I wanted to change the energy and go with something slower and more profound for the new short program. "Caravan" had a lot of flair, with showy choreography to match the trills of the brass instruments, so we decided to create a more subtle, introspective program. She wanted to explore a more romantic side of my skating, and she played a bunch of more emotive pieces from her database of music that she had earmarked for me. I'm pretty picky when it comes to selecting the right song to skate to when provided options, but that season, when she played "La Bohème" by Charles Aznavour, it immediately stood out. It sounded unique and beautiful and authentic, so it was an easy selection.

The melancholy mood of the piece was particularly poignant for Shae at the time. A year earlier, skater Denis Ten was killed while being robbed in his hometown of Almaty, Kazakhstan. Denis was an amazing athlete who had won the bronze at the 2014 Sochi Olympics in men's singles, and he had been training in Lake Arrowhead with Frank Carroll when I first moved to California. Shae was close to Denis, and so many in the figure skating world were shocked by his death.

The concept of death was really prominent in her mind as she choreographed the "La Bohème" program, and the sentimentality of the song, in which Aznavour reminisces longingly for the bohemian lifestyle that artists lived in Paris, really meshed well with her grief. We talked a lot about how fleeting life was and how Aznavour's lyrics really focused on the importance of recognizing and holding on to beauty wherever and whenever you experienced it, because it doesn't last. In the song, he revisits some of his favorite places around Montmartre and finds that the cafés and studio where he once painted were gone, and yearns for his youth and the innocence of that time.

As I said, a definite 180 from the upbeat "Caravan" from the year before, but I was also ready to take my skating in a new direction and tell a more emotive story on the ice. Although we didn't want the piece to focus as much on death as on longing, the mood was more somber and serious.

Making that connection, and exploring the dueling themes of appreciating life while accepting change and death as an integral part of life, gave the program more depth; and on a personal level, made me appreciate the people in my life even more. That helped me to continue developing the character I played in the program. One of the things I enjoy about skating is the opportunity to adapt different characters and show emotions that you wouldn't necessarily express yourself, and that was certainly the case for me with "La Bohème."

Marie was also up for a change from the epic grandeur of Woodkid, and she had just the piece in mind. She had started choreographing a program to some Elton John songs from the movie *Rocketman* for one of her dance teams, but she saved some selections she thought would work for me. By the time I got to Montreal, she was excited for me to hear both the music and her ideas for a program. As soon as I listened to the music, I knew it was perfect. It was completely different from my short program, which was a deciding factor for me—I never want two programs that are too similar. I had also watched *Rocketman* and really enjoyed it. I thought the movie did a good job of portraying the personal challenges Elton John went through to pursue his music and how dedicated he remained to himself and his craft.

The goal with the *Rocketman* program was to use a medley of Elton John songs and build from a slower-paced song to the exciting, faster pace of "Rocket Man" and "Bennie and the Jets." The first part of the program, to "Goodbye Yellow Brick Road," almost borrows a bit from my short program, with the feeling of longing for something that's changed or someone who's leaving. Marie and I felt the transition was a cool way to tie in the concept of understanding who you are before you can finally break free—which in the program occurs when "Rocket Man" comes on.

To complete the package, Vera Wang again designed amazing costumes for those programs. After hearing about "La Bohème," she wanted something that conveyed romanticism, to pick up on the feeling that pervades Aznavour's song. She interpreted the romantic feeling of that program as a color, and designed a silky lavender top for me that was simple, comfortable, and was very symbolic of the feeling behind the song.

For "Rocket Man," she wanted something that really stood out and gravitated toward a neon color to go with the song's otherworldly focus. Vera pays a lot of attention to what other skaters are wearing and always wants me to stand out. She thought my long program needed an outfit that really popped. She was into lettering and wanted to include blocky letters to provide a visual focal point. She suggested "Nathan," or even a "C," but I felt a little shy about that so we settled on "E" for Elton, which was on the sleeve of the bright greenish-yellow top. Vera and her team always custom-make all the prints on the fabrics of my costumes, so they are unique and special. And she also started to add a meaningful touch for me—she sewed a little red tag into my costumes because in Chinese culture, red symbolizes luck and happiness, and represents life and vitality. I really appreciated that extra care she put into everything she made for me.

None of us had any way of knowing then that we had just choreographed my two programs for the 2022 Winter Olympics, which were still two years away. We also had no way of knowing how dramatically the world would change over the next two years and how all the plans we had made would be turned upside down.

6 PANDEMIC

兵来将挡水来土掩

Fight the invaders with army and stop the flood with earth.

When I headed back to school in September 2019, I knew I had a big decision to make: how much time I needed to take off from Yale to train for the 2022 Winter Olympics. I wanted to take at least a year off, and possibly two, so I could go back to California to focus exclusively on training. Considering how quickly the technical bar had risen from 2014 to 2018, it was a pretty good bet that in the next three years we were going to see even higher skill levels.

After talking to my advisers at Yale, I had two options. I could go to school for two years and then take two years off to train. Every student is allowed to take off only one full year, or two semesters. If I wanted to take two years off, I would have to formally withdraw, then reapply to request getting reinstated after 2022.

But Raf wanted me to come back as soon as I could, reiterating that it was okay to keep my skills where they were in the first two years of an Olympic cycle, but he strongly advised that I spend at least two years focusing exclusively on training so that I could continue improving the consistency and quality of my elements beyond where I had stood in the previous Olympic cycle. My parents supported me either way. I started looking into the process of withdrawing so I could take two years off, and worked with my adviser to learn more about the logistics. Basically it boiled down to maintaining a certain academic level, or passing a specific number of classes. Other than that, from what I could tell, it didn't seem too complicated. As long as I passed all my classes, I could email my residential college dean with a request to withdraw. Then the academic board would review my request and make the final decision.

Before my semester ended, my family, Raf, and I decided that getting back to California for two years would be the best option for me to prepare for the 2022 Winter Olympics, so I sent an email to my dean, letting her know that I planned to send her my withdrawal request. But as it turned out, I didn't have to go through the process of withdrawing and getting reinstated after all.

After the Christmas and New Year's holidays, I came back to campus in January 2020 just as COVID-19 arrived in the United States. Soon the virus was spreading quickly around the world. There were rumors around campus that Yale was going to close, but no one had any idea what was going to happen. After Nationals ended on January 26, I returned to campus and continued going to classes. When spring recess started on March 6, most students had left campus. I stayed, as I had the previous year, to take advantage of the empty Whale and additional ice time to train for the World Championships.

On March 10, all students got an email telling us not to come back to campus. Our classes switched to online. My residential college dean then explained to me that, because of the pandemic, Yale would give all students an extra year off. This made my decision to train much easier: I was allowed one year more away from school in addition to the year I was already granted as a student. I was all set to train for two years back in California with Raf.

The World Championships were scheduled to start on March 16 in Montreal, Canada, but on March 11, the International Skating Union canceled the competition, only the fourth time that the event wasn't held since it debuted in 1896. They were canceled during World War I and World War II and in 1961, when a plane crash killed the entire U.S. Figure Skating team traveling to the competition. Now ISU officials decided it was too risky to hold the event and gather dozens of skaters from around the world in one place.

That day, I packed up all of my skating stuff from the Whale. I decided to help out a friend of mine who coached at Champions Skating Center by working with his students on jump technique. Not long after, Tony called and said that spending time with so many different people probably wasn't a good idea since the virus was spreading, and that I should try to minimize contact with others to avoid getting infected. My parents had moved to Colorado by this time, so I planned to head back home for spring break. Tony called again and said that if I flew home to Colorado I might expose my parents to the virus from my travels since COVID-19 cases were rising, so I decided to go straight to California for training.

Because everything happened so quickly, I still didn't have a place to live in Orange County. Before I had left for Yale, my mom and I had been renting a little apartment in Long Beach, which was about an hour's drive from the Great Park rink in Irvine, where I trained. My mom initially kept the lease after I left, but when I came back west during winter break my first year, we realized it was too long a drive from the apartment to the rink, so my mom didn't renew the lease and went back to Colorado Springs to be with my dad.

I stayed in two different Airbnbs close to Great Park, for about a month. I was living out of my suitcase because a lot of my stuff was either in storage or in Colorado with my parents, or back at Yale. The university allowed students to come back to campus to pick up their stuff over a designated week that spring, but I wasn't able to so the school ended up shipping all my belongings back to me.

I thought I could skate once I got to Great Park, but as more

COVID-19 cases were reported in the United States, cities and states started to lock down, closing schools, restaurants, and other businesses. The rink was no exception. That ended up being okay, since the spring and summer make up the off-season, and I usually rest and recover then, and don't spend as much time on the ice. Normally I would be touring in shows, in both Japan and the United States. But those were canceled, too.

California ended up going into a strict lockdown, so I chilled in the Airbnb, which was a room in a family's home. I cooked for myself but didn't have to worry about basic supplies like toilet paper when everyone else was emptying store shelves. But the family had relatives visit from time to time so I got a little uncomfortable with potentially getting exposed to COVID-19, and I moved to another Airbnb where I lived alone.

Even though I wasn't skating, I had plenty to do. After spring recess was over, our classes resumed online, so I still had to complete the school year. I liked being able to concentrate entirely on school and not have to juggle the crazy schedule I had back in New Haven. But Raf knew I was back in California, and he called my mom, asking when I would be back to train, even if it was off ice. I told him I'd be focused on finishing my schoolwork until the semester was over.

Schoolwork distracted me from worrying too much about how COVID-19 would affect my training for the upcoming season, or even the Olympics. Nobody knew how long the lockdowns and the other disruptions would last. Like everyone else, I kind of assumed the pandemic would be over in a few weeks, or months at the most. I had no way of knowing we would still be dealing with COVID-19 and the massive changes it would cause—testing and masking and competing in a bubble—all the way through the 2022 Beijing Winter Olympics.

Raf urged my mom to come out to California with me. I think

he was hoping she would prod me into starting off-ice training. My family thought it was too risky for her to be on a plane. I agreed, and I, too, was really careful and essentially kept to myself in the Airbnb and didn't see many people in order to lower my risk of getting infected.

As soon as the semester ended, I contacted Raf and told him I was ready to start getting back into shape. By this time, I had been off the ice for a month and didn't feel I was strong enough to start skating again. If I had gotten on the ice immediately, I probably would have hurt myself. Raf's first objective was to get me strong again, but the gyms were closed. He, Mariah Bell, another of the skaters he was coaching, and I would meet for outdoor activities at different parks, even at the local tennis courts. Raf believed that playing different sports helped skaters to be more mobile and flexible so we had fun facing off across the tennis net. We'd also do some off-ice jumps, to work on getting my muscles back into the habit of skating.

I also reached out to Brandon Siakel, and things really fell into place. His girlfriend was living in Los Angeles. Just before the lockdown, he had left Colorado Springs, where he was based, to visit her in LA for two weeks. When things shut down and travel was limited, his bosses told him to stay in LA and work with athletes there. He borrowed a bunch of equipment from a friend of ours, Tyler Poor, who was a strength and conditioning coach at Lakewood where we used to train. Tyler's gym was too far from Great Park, so Brandon basically carried a mobile gym in the trunk of his girlfriend's car (weights, a trap bar, bands, and weighted vests). Mariah and I would meet Brandon in the park for sessions three days a week. I'm sure we looked interesting going through our exercises next to families, whose kids were running around and playing in the park.

That went on for about a month before the officials at Great Park finally were allowed to let a few skaters, including me, Mariah, and

Raf, back in the rink. We had to wear masks and socially distance, but it was great to get back on the ice. A few weeks later, the rink allowed only four or five people on the ice at any one time to make sure everyone was safe.

After being off the ice for a while, getting back to skating isn't just a matter of picking up where you left off. In the entire seventeen years I had been skating, I had taken only a couple of days off to rest, except in 2012 when I was dealing with my ankle injury and 2016 when I had my hip surgery. Aside from that, this was the longest time I had been off the ice. So I couldn't immediately go back to skating three to four hours a day, as I had been doing. I could maybe skate one or two hours a day, and that was a perfect way to get back in skating shape. Rafael and I took this time to break down my technique and work on the basics. When I got back to jumping, I had to monitor how many jumps I did a day. In my mind I knew how to jump, but my muscles were slower to respond because of the time away. Thankfully things came back fairly quickly, although it was an unusual experience because my body felt so weak and so heavy. Things that normally were quick and easy took a lot more reps. And at the end of the day, even if I hadn't done much, I was exhausted and my legs were tired.

That was the hardest part—building day by day back to the place where I was able to do quads again and then put them together like I needed to in a program. It took a few months before that happened, too. After jumps being second nature for years, it was strange to lose them temporarily and have to build them back.

By this time, my mom had done her usual thorough online search and found an apartment for us in a complex a few miles from the rink.

COVID-19 was certainly throwing a lot of uncertainty into everyone's lives. For athletes, there was a lot of turmoil that sprung around what would happen with the Summer Olympic Games that were scheduled for July 2020 in Tokyo. Officials were talking about the possibility that the Summer Games would get either canceled or postponed by a few months or a whole year. Either way, it would be challenging for all the athletes who were training; I know how carefully athletes plan how they progress in order to be in peak shape at the Olympics. I was keeping close track of the news about this, since it could also affect the Winter Games two years away, in 2022. When the International Olympic Committee decided in March 2020 to postpone the Tokyo Games for a year I was actually relieved, because the Games hadn't been canceled. I thought, "Okay there's still hope for 2022 because the Winter Games are so soon after the Summer Games, and if the Summer Games can be hosted we will be on track to start on schedule."

But Michal Březina wasn't as optimistic. He thought 2022 wasn't going to happen as scheduled and would also probably be postponed since it was only six months after the Summer Games. I really hoped he was wrong, because everything had worked out so well in terms of my time away from Yale. I didn't want to have to deal with the whole withdrawal process if I had to train for a third year. If the Olympics went on as scheduled, I could go straight back to school in fall 2022. If the Games were postponed, it would definitely be a roadblock.

I tried my best not to think about that too much though, since it was out of my control.

As the summer wore on, COVID-19 was looming larger and larger over the world, and it didn't look like things were going back to normal anytime soon. It certainly started to seem like the next skating season might be affected by the pandemic, too.

Now that I had a place to live, my mom came back to California to help me move in and get settled. But I was really worried about her safety and I didn't want her to get sick. The day she came I was so scared that I Cloroxed every surface in the apartment about four times, and I wore gloves and masks every time I left the place. I had a lot of anxiety, because at that time I didn't know how COVID would affect me or how severe the disease was. I knew people were getting really sick and going on ventilators, and a lot of people were dying. My objective was to quarantine as much as I could and to avoid people I didn't know as much as I could. Whenever I did anything outside the rink with Raf, we would make sure it was outdoors.

Our rink was great about limiting people who were allowed in and about sanitizing everything. The rink also required all the skaters to answer a health questionnaire daily, have their temperature checked at the entrance of the facility, and to wear a mask in the facility and on the ice.

All those precautions were worth it, because we were very lucky that we had very few cases at the rink, so we felt pretty protected from getting the virus. Of course, we weren't going out to eat and I wasn't even going anywhere where they offered outdoor dining. I ended up spending a lot of time in the apartment with my mom. It turned out to be a great opportunity to brush up on my Chinese. I could understand it and speak a little, so I figured that since the Games were going to be in Beijing, I might as well get a little better at familiarizing myself with Chinese—and I already had a teacher in my mom. She asked her brother in China to send some elementary school text and reading books to help me learn the language and increase my Chinese vocabulary. Since Chinese characters are pretty complex, my mom would write out the phonetic version in the Roman alphabet, called pinyin, for me and I would read that. I'm far from fluent but feel like I could probably get by in China in a pinch.

My mom was really happy about the extra time we got to spend together during those months. I also suggested that we start playing chess, which we did in the evenings. My brothers and sisters are much better players than I am, but I had picked it up as well and tried to improve on my skills.

When I wasn't in the apartment, I hung out with Mariah and Michal Březina and his wife a lot, going to the beach and spending time at their places. We tended to stick together because we didn't want to be around people we didn't know; and we trusted that each of us were taking all the precautions against COVID-19 and being responsible about not putting ourselves at risk. We couldn't stay cooped up in our apartments all the time, so it was nice to be able to spend time with other people in a safe way. Michal and his wife also had had a baby that February, so they were extra worried about potentially bringing the virus home to their daughter. We ended up becoming really close during this time, and it was nice to have other skaters who understood the pressure and frustration of what it took to train for the Olympics, especially during a pandemic.

At that point I wasn't even thinking about the season, because basically there was no season. The only thing we generally attend toward the end of the summer is Champs Camp, during which the U.S. skating team gets together along with judges and officials to get feedback on our programs for the upcoming season to make sure we are prepared. Basically if you don't go to Champs Camp, then you don't compete in the Grand Prix series.

Given all the uncertainty with the season, I asked Mitch Moyer at U.S. Figure Skating whether we were going to have Champs Camp that year, and he said he didn't know. Ultimately, U.S. Figure Skating decided to hold the camp, but virtually. All the skaters submitted videos that we took on our phones at a specific time, showing the time stamp on it to prove that it was filmed in one take. We had to submit the videos by a certain time and have them reviewed by the judges. I did that for my short and free programs. It was an interesting way to perform, but I figured it was a harbinger of how the season was going to look. And having a remote session was better than not having any feedback on my skating at all.

Even though nobody knew what would happen with the upcoming season, I continued to train, because whether or not the competitions would be held, or whether they would be in person or virtual, I had to be ready.

The pandemic also gave Brandon and me a chance to spend more time experimenting with a more quantifiable way to measure my training and how much it was stressing my hip and related muscles. A friend of Brandon's who worked with a strength and conditioning coach in Major League Baseball told him about a sensor that measured the velocity of batters' swings and pitchers' throws. Brandon worked with U.S. Figure Skating and the USOPC to get a grant to buy the system. A sports scientist with U.S. Figure Skating then engineered a version that was calibrated for skaters' jumps and spins. Soon after we got back into the rink after quarantine, I wore the sensor on my hip and started collecting data on how much "work" I was doing during each training session. It was more quantitative than the formulas Brandon and I had tried to come up with, and that made it easier for me to make use of it. The sensor sent data to an app on my phone, which helped me to target the sweet spot number of jumps that would give me enough repetitions without causing my hip to flare up again. I've heard that other U.S. skaters competing in the Grand Prix series have also used it, including those who trained at the U.S. Olympic & Paralympic Training Center in Colorado Springs.

By this time, Shae-Lynn Bourne had moved to Los Angeles, so we began working on my programs for the coming season; she choreographed both my short and free programs that year. The free that Shae choreographed became one of my favorite programs, to selections from Philip Glass's works, because I felt his minimalist style really drove us to be more creative and expressive with my movements on the ice.

In August 2020, the International Skating Union confirmed that the Grand Prix series would proceed as planned. But because of the dynamic situation with the surge in COVID-19 cases, it also allowed each skating federation in the country where an event was held to decide whether or not to go ahead with the competition, depending on how comfortable they were with the number of COVID-19 cases in their country. That year, the final was supposed to be held in Beijing, at Capital Indoor Stadium, where the Olympic figure skating competition would take place, as a test event for the 2022 Winter Olympics. Because of COVID-19, however, the ISU said it would decide later in the season whether or not the final would be held. And for each of the six events, no skaters from outside the country where it was held could compete, since many countries had travel restrictions in place at the time. So, instead of being assigned to two events, most of us had the opportunity to skate in just a single Grand Prix competition in or near our home country.

Then, in October 2020, the skating federations in France and Canada announced that they were canceling their events, leaving four of the six competitions in the series.

I was assigned to compete at Skate America in October. I was still worried about COVID-19 but had several reasons for wanting to compete. With the Grand Prix Final still up in the air, I felt that this might be my only opportunity to compete that season. Plus, it was the year before the Olympics, and I wanted to see where I needed to improve, and to compete as much as I could in order to prepare and be at my peak for the Games. I didn't know if I would have another chance to compete in person, so I felt that it was better to go and see what happened. There was also a team competition at the end of Skate America, so it was a chance to have back-to-back events when we didn't know when the next one would be.

Before we even left, we were getting a lot of information from U.S. Figure Skating, which was hosting the event, about what they were doing to make sure that everyone was safe.

They put into place a strict testing policy. We had to get a PCR test before we left and show that we were negative; and once we got to the competition, we would be tested again and have to quarantine in our rooms until we got our results. If we tested negative, we could leave our rooms. There would be no audience, and the competition was being held in a bubble. Anyone associated with the event had to get tested regularly and couldn't leave the bubble until their confirmed departure date. In addition, U.S. Figure Skating had very strict rules about not interacting with people not linked to the event.

I felt safe going into the competition. The stakes seemed low enough for the risk we were taking on. Since there wasn't going to be an audience and the attendees would continue to test after returning home, the likelihood of the event becoming a super-spreader was fairly low.

My concern about COVID-19 was changing as the pandemic changed. At the beginning, when I had no idea what COVID-19 was, I had a lot of fear and anxiety about it, as did everyone else. For example, when I was flying back to California from New Haven in March, there were only a couple of hundred cases in the United States, but I wore an N95 mask and brought sanitizing wipes with me and cleaned everything around my seat. The more familiar I got with what I could do to protect myself, the more my worry receded.

Janice also helped a lot. She became my go-to person for all things COVID-19. She has a PhD in molecular and cell biology, worked in the lab of Nobel laureate Jennifer Doudna at the University of California Berkeley, and cofounded a biotech company, Mammoth Biosciences, so whenever I had a question about COVID-19, I texted her. She drilled into me that wearing a mask was my best defense, and recommended that I wear an N95 mask early on. She really helped me to understand how to control the things that I could control about the virus, so that the unknowns didn't consume me.

By the fall of 2020, after nearly seven months of being isolated, I really embraced the opportunity to compete. We didn't know if we would have National Championships or which of the remaining Grand Prix events would be held. My last competition had been Nationals in January 2020, and Raf was also eager for us to compete.

Once we got to Skate America, U.S. Figure Skating did a great job of putting a lot of safety restrictions in place for us. It was the first time I competed with COVID-19 rules, so it was an all new experience, but I didn't mind. We could enter and exit the hotel only from a designated doorway, which was separate from the one everyone else not associated with the event used. It led straight to the arena that was connected to the hotel. The system kept us in as much of a bubble as possible.

The strangest thing at that competition was skating without an audience. It was kind of nice in the sense that it felt similar to a practice, except with the judging panel in front of you. There were some people in the stands—the skaters competing in the other disciplines—but we were only allowed in the suites, so there was no one sitting in the lower level closest to the ice. The environment was nowhere near that of an actual competition. When I walked into the arena from backstage toward the ice, I was confused for a moment to see faces in the seats, but what I thought was a crowd turned out to be cardboard cutouts. I later learned this was a fundraiser from supportive skating fans around the world for the U.S.

Figure Skating Memorial Fund, created after the tragic 1961 plane crash. The fund provides scholarships to qualified young athletes; I am grateful to have benefited from the Memorial Fund throughout my career.

The audience has a huge impact on how a competition feels. I don't necessarily hear everything in the crowd when I'm competing, but I feel the energy. When there's a big audience, my adrenaline starts flowing. At this competition, the atmosphere felt especially different when I went to do my elements. After landing a jump, I expected to hear a reaction from the stands, but instead there was dead silence. U.S. Figure Skating decided to play canned applause but only at the ends of our programs. It was strange, but would become "normal" over the next two years.

Even though that competition seemed more like a test event, I still felt that internal pressure to try and perform as well as I could to get a score I would be happy with. There were a lot of cobwebs to shake off since I hadn't competed in so long—things like the logistics of planning what I needed to do in the twenty-minute warm-up in the morning before the competition and then what I needed to do during my six-minute warm-up just before my group skated. Because it had been a while, it all felt new. But once I got into the flow of things, it was like riding a bicycle: I knew what I had to do, but I was a little rusty.

My short program was okay: I landed a quad toe with a triple toe in combination, and a quad flip. But my free was shakier than I would have liked. I landed three quads but doubled my planned quad Salchow and popped my triple Axel. I did the quad loop in the free program of the team competition, though, so I was happy about that. Overall, I skated the way that I expected, which was both a good thing and a bad thing. I wasn't ready to perform at the elite level where I wanted to be, but the things I had been working on—basic skating skills, jump timing, jump patterns—were getting there.

My stamina and strength still needed a lot of work, which meant my consistency and quality weren't fully on display. That wasn't a surprise, given the longer than usual off-season. Looking back, I went into that first competition, a year and a half before the 2022 Winter Olympics, a lot more relaxed than I would have had there been no COVID-19. In the year before an Olympics, there generally isn't enough time to focus on the basics. The goal is less to learn new material and more to hone the skills you already have so they can be perfect at the Games. But because we had had so much time off the ice before the 2020–2021 season, I could give myself more time to take a step back to conceptualize and learn new things without feeling stressed or under a time crunch. It was an exciting learning process that benefited my skating in the long run.

However, as different as the pandemic made things for competing, I also know and appreciate that for us as athletes, it could have been a lot worse, especially for me. I was very fortunate: all my friends and my family are safe, none of them got especially ill, none had to go to the hospital, none went to the emergency room, none of us were put in the ICU, and none of us really lost our jobs. I know from the news how hard the pandemic hit people, so I'm not in a position to complain. I still had the ability to train, and I still had the ability to go to competitions. I know that I'm lucky, and I'm extremely grateful for that.

Competing wasn't the only thing we had to worry about at the event. Toward the end of Skate America, it seemed like the whole of California was catching on fire; it was a record-breaking year when it came to forest fires. During the competition, several huge fires broke out in Orange County, where we trained, affecting dozens of acres. As the competition went on, the other skaters from our rink and I grew less concerned about the competition and more worried about whether we would have homes to return to or whether we would need to leave Skate America early to evacuate and move all our stuff out.

As the fires raged on, we learned the residents in our apartment complex were ordered to evacuate. By the end of the competition, the evacuation order remained in place. So Kaitlin Hawayek, an ice dancer who was at Skate America, and Mariah and I ended up going to San Diego for a night after we finished competing. I stayed with my brother Tony and crashed on his sofa before I drove back home the next day. Fortunately, our building was spared from the fires, and while there was a lot of smoke for a few days, we were lucky that we ended up largely unaffected.

A few weeks before the Grand Prix Final, scheduled for December 2020 in Beijing, the ISU canceled the competition. That meant I would have only one more chance to compete, at the U.S. National Championships in January 2021, before the World Championships in March, which were scheduled for Stockholm, Sweden.

I skated pretty well at Nationals, then immediately focused on the upcoming Worlds. Raf and I make a lot of our decisions about which jumps I will do based on the competition I'm facing. Raf insisted that I should try to push for improving my technical content by putting a quad flip–triple toe combination in the second half of my short program, since in previous seasons my second half jump combination had been the easier quad toe–triple toe. With so few competitions, and so much uncertainty about which events would actually be held, I didn't have the option to slowly build this layout in from event-to-event. Raf and I felt it was important for me to keep being competitive as we built toward Beijing, this was a calculated risk that he thought would challenge me and prepare me for the Games.

My free program performance at Worlds in Stockholm was strong—Raf later said he thought it was among the best he saw from me leading up to Beijing. He attributed that to our work over the summer that focused on creating more freedom and flow in my technique to make my jumps as easy and strong as possible. The competition didn't start off well though, with a fall on my opening quad Lutz in the short program, which put me in third behind Yuzuru and his teammate Yuma Kagiyama, a really talented young skater who was clearly going to be a medal contender at the Olympics. I think I needed time to shake off the nerves of competing at Worlds again.

I was upset with the way I skated in the short, and felt similar to the way I had after my short programs in 2018. I again went into the free program feeling I had nothing to lose. Without the additional pressure, I felt unusually calm and ready. I ended up rallying and managed to land five quads. Raf was proud of the way I was able to come back and win that competition; I was proud, too. I don't generally go back and watch my programs except when I want to study them to find ways to improve, but that free program is one of the few that I can look back on fondly, with few criticisms of my skating.

Skating well was only part of the challenge all of us were facing at Worlds. The pandemic still overshadowed competitions and our training; some athletes, like me, were fortunate enough to have been spared while others got sick. I wanted to know how big an impact it would have on my training if I were to get infected, so I asked the athletes who had gotten sick if the virus had wiped them out or whether they were able to recover pretty quickly. They all said getting COVID-19 was terrible and that it prevented them from training; some said that they still struggled with fatigue and stamina issues weeks and months later.

Most of the athletes who got COVID-19 at that time had been affected by the Delta variant, which seemed to be a pretty serious strain. Because people were starting to get vaccinated, the mortality rate was lower, and the immunity provided by the vaccines appeared to be holding up. But getting infected could still wipe you out for a few days, if not longer, and negatively impact training. So many of the skaters who got sick at that time struggled with breathing after they resumed training, which was a concern for me.

After some time, the Omicron strain replaced Delta. It was more transmissible, so you were more likely to get infected. If you were, though, it didn't seem like you would get seriously ill, particularly if you were vaccinated. At that point, I was starting to worry about the extensive testing at events and the possibility of testing positive and, even if I felt fine, not being able to compete. That would have been a nightmare situation for me. I needed to compete in order to be as prepared as I could for Beijing. It was terrifying to think that I might test positive, not be able to travel to events, and not be able to compete: all my preparation would be worthless. If I couldn't compete, what was I doing all this for?

I did everything I could to protect myself, including getting vaccinated as soon as I was eligible, after April 2021. My mom and I went to an outdoor vaccination site set up by Los Angeles County and got our shots around the same time. It gave us a little more peace of mind, but we continued to wear masks and keep to ourselves so we wouldn't get exposed.

I watched the Summer Olympics in July and August 2021 very closely. Whatever happened there would serve as a bellwether for the Beijing Olympics. It was nerve-racking, because the Tokyo Olympics was the first large international sports event where athletes and media from around the world would be gathering during the pandemic. I was really hoping there wouldn't be large outbreaks and that the Games wouldn't become a super-spreader event. If it did, that would almost certainly affect the Beijing Olympics, which were supposed to take place just six months later—and might even put them in danger of being canceled.

I also knew that whatever testing and prevention measures that the Tokyo Olympic Committee put in place would likely set precedent for the Beijing Olympic officials, so it would give me a sense of what hurdles I might have to face. Fortunately, the Japanese Olympic Committee did a good job of testing regularly and keeping everyone in a semi-bubble; and there wasn't a large number of cases linked to the Olympics that summer.

Ultimately, while I was worried about whether the Winter Games would happen, I accepted that it was out of my control. All I could do was stay focused and keep training as if they were going ahead as scheduled.

7 BUILDING RESILIENCE

一个篱笆三个桩, 一个好汉三个帮

A fence needs three poles and a hero needs three helpers.

The buildup of pressure and tension leading up to an Olympic season always takes its toll—not just on me but also on the people I'm closest to. That was especially true of my relationship with my mom. Over the course of my career, the relationship I had with my mom was constantly changing, particularly after the two years I spent at Yale. I could never have become an Olympian without my mom. But as with any close and intense relationship, it wasn't always a smooth and easy journey.

I know it's not conventional that my mom was such an integral part of my skating training. And some people might assume that she is the stereotypical Chinese tiger mom who pushes her kids and drives them really hard, with little regard for what they want. To a certain extent that's true—she always wants us to work hard—but not without regard for what we want. She pushes us so we can enjoy the rewards of all that effort. From the start, she wanted us to appreciate everything we had, and make the most of any opportunities that came to us. Which is why, if we took lessons, she wanted us to learn from them, so we didn't waste the time and effort we put into them.

But I always knew that she would never force us to participate in any activity if we didn't find it fulfilling or engaging. If we did decide to pursue something, however, we only had one choice, and that was to give it our complete attention and effort and learn how to weather any challenges we might face. She would often say to me, "It is better to struggle and cry before competition than to struggle and cry after competition." I found that a little humorous, but I loved the practicality embedded in it. It gave me the freedom to know that practice won't always be perfect, but the accomplishments that can be achieved and the strength built from persevering will justify and diminish any pain that comes from the challenges.

It's funny—when I saw the Pixar movie *Turning Red*, which is about the expectations that Asian parents have for their children, a lot of the scenes were really relatable for me. I'm sure they are for a lot of other first-generation children of immigrants. Because my parents sacrificed so much for my siblings and me, and experienced such hardships, that pushing, even if it sometimes feels overbearing, comes from good intentions. That's just the love language of Asian parents—alongside preparing fresh cut fruit for you at the end of the day. (That's an Asian thing, by the way, and one I really am fond of. Try it; it's a great way to finish off dinner.) They want us to avoid the struggles they experienced because they couldn't speak the language or didn't have the same opportunities we do to pursue what we love and to work hard to achieve our dreams.

My Chinese mom's parenting style wasn't always smooth sailing. When I was young, her hands-on approach wasn't well-received at the rink; management started implementing new rules, first to prevent her from working with me, and eventually to prevent her from speaking with me entirely while inside the rink. But that only fueled her motivation further. She believes the best way to counter negativity is to focus on working even harder and getting even better.

Now that I'm old enough, I can appreciate how much she gave up for us, and how hard it must have been for her to make sure all of us could have the opportunities that we did. My sisters and brothers and I never felt anything was out of reach if we wanted to try it as kids. If my sisters wanted to take dance classes, my mom found scholarships or took on extra jobs to pay for them. The same was true for my skating classes.

When my mom pushed me to work harder and packed my days with training, lessons, and homework, sometimes I felt overwhelmed. So when I started getting more experienced, I wanted more autonomy over my skating and my life. Up to that point, my mom perfectly filled the role that I needed her to play. As my de facto trainer, she organized and directed the logistics of my days. But especially after being at Yale, I felt I had accumulated enough experience to start managing my schedule and my training on my own. Granted, I was still relatively inexperienced and impatient, and if I had truly been left to my own devices, who knows where my skating would have ended up. My mom is an extremely caring person, but she believed that work was work, and when you had a job to do, nothing else mattered. Her philosophy is not to highlight the things I did well, since I had already mastered them, but to focus on things that still needed improving. For much of my skating career, however, I interpreted that as not being good enough, which sometimes caused frustration.

My mom became my de facto head coach not only because she wanted to but really also because she had to. Raf wanted me to learn independence; that didn't happen overnight but took many years. In the meantime, rather than adding yet another person to the team to oversee my training, my mom was already in a good place to pick up that role. She studied my lessons with Stephanee, Karel, and Genia closely, acting as their proxy for the rest of the time I spent on the ice outside of lessons. So while Raf has the official name of head coach, I kind of always saw my mom in that role. She was in charge of structuring my practices and working out my day-to-day routines, minus the detailed skating technique, of course. It was never in writing, or explicitly determined that she was my training coach, but that's the way it had always been.

When we lived in the tiny cabin in Lake Arrowhead, she had a whiteboard that kept track of my daily practices and jumps, and essentially laid out the recipe for my skating success. And when I was younger, I followed what she and my coaches told me to do. I honestly didn't mind her doing that, even if she pushed me really hard at times. I just assumed that as the adult, she knew best and my job was to follow her advice. And I figured that I needed to be pushed, because if I didn't have someone providing some type of structure in my life, I wouldn't be disciplined enough to train as much as I needed to.

For a lot of my skating career, my confidence was based on whether my mom was confident. And she was confident only when I practiced a lot. Her philosophy was that no matter what happened in a competition—whether I got nervous, or I was skating with some pain because of a minor injury—if I trained hard enough, my body would take over and my muscle memory would get me through. For her, everything depended on training, and training a lot.

But as I got older, I began to accumulate skating experiences that she could not. Athletics can be an all-consuming pursuit, and maintaining that high level of intensity outside of the rink can be draining. One of my mom's greatest attributes is her mental ability to persevere and stop at nothing to obtain a goal. Maybe this comes from her experience as an immigrant, making a life in a new and unfamiliar country. I didn't always see the need to take things to the highest gear at which she seemed to operate. Sometimes it could become exhausting when my mistakes and tough practices on the ice would follow me into our conversations at home. To be fair, though, there was no other place she could really talk to me about that since we couldn't discuss my skating at the rink like my coaches did.

The relationships between a parent and child, and between a coach and a skater, are inherently two very different interactions; when there is overlap, as there was with my mom and me, it naturally becomes difficult to navigate.

After two years at Yale, balancing school and skating, I had learned a few things about what training regimen worked for me, and that didn't always involve training full steam ahead all the time. In addition, because of my hip, I was paying closer attention to how intensely I was training and learning to adjust the training load depending on how close I was to competing.

Ultimately, we wanted the same goal, which was for me to be prepared so I could perform my best; it's just that we had very different ways of getting there. My mom felt that everything I did, including how I spent my time off the ice, should be in some way beneficial for my training. However, I was beginning to realize that in order to maximize my efficiency on the ice, I needed the space and time to decompress away from the sport.

I understood where my mom was coming from. She really enjoyed studying biographies of successful athletes, as well as textbooks on training methods. It didn't matter which sport they played— baseball, basketball, swimming, golf, football, or hockey—she read about them all. She even read books by championship coaches. What she got from their stories was one thing: in order to succeed, you need to work hard and to make sacrifices. To become a champion, you have to push yourself harder and further than your competitors. We spent a lot of time debating her perception of my motivation, or lack thereof. I felt I needed to find a balance between skating and the rest of my life; she thought that without making sacrifices in the other parts of my life, I wouldn't become a champion. There was no right answer, of course, but we were learning that we needed to find a compromise between our differing viewpoints.

In order to be successful, I felt I needed to be able to go to the rink refreshed, energized, and happy. I trusted my ability to train and prepare for competitions, which meant intensifying my focus in the weeks leading up to an event, rather than training at 100 percent the entire season, which I knew would lead to burnout. My mom knew from my past experiences that there were unexpected issues that would emerge—I would get injured or sick, or have a problem with my skating boots—that would hinder my training and force me to take time off. So she believed I needed to maximize every second of every day I did train so that if I couldn't avoid taking time off the ice, I would still be properly prepared.

It took many discussions to find the common ground in our training philosophies. We ultimately agreed that in long stretches preceding my competitions, I would be responsible for my daily training and she wouldn't come to the rink. That way, I could trust my own body and mind to dictate how many repetitions, and how many program run-throughs I felt I needed. Closer to the competition, she would come to the rink and serve as my quality control, providing feedback on areas where I needed to refine my performance more. This ended up being the perfect compromise to allow me enough autonomy to build my confidence, while giving me the mental break from skating when I was at home with her since she wasn't monitoring my daily progress.

Still, getting there was a journey, and we had some pretty intense arguments, which were usually triggered when I came home past my curfew, got on the ice a few minutes late, or took some time away from skating. Discipline was so important to my mom, and she felt it was the key to helping me prepare for Beijing. Without discipline, she believed success would be nearly impossible for me to achieve. And she wasn't just focused on discipline at the rink; my recovery and nutrition all required that same level of dedication. While I agreed with her in principle, I found it unsustainable. I struggled with the fact that everything about our relationship was about my skating, and I sometimes just wanted to be mom and son. The times we spent together interacting that way, we would go on hikes, play tennis, shoot hoops (she would be my rebounder) and throw the football (she throws a pretty mean spiral), and talk about things other than skating, which I enjoyed. But when we reverted to my training, I would get frustrated because after having spent the entire day at the rink, I wanted to talk about anything but that. I know she only wanted me to have a better training session the next day and every day after that, but I couldn't always accept that. And don't get me wrong—she has helped me tremendously on improving my skating because she has a good eye for what I'm doing wrong and bad habits I might be picking up—I just wasn't always ready for her high level of discipline all the time.

Ultimately, I learned to accept that all aspects of my life—including my relationships with my family—were intimately tied to skating, and there was no way to avoid it. And I know that she was damn good at being my training coach. Without her, I wouldn't have spent hours watching videos of my mistakes so that I could fix them and keep improving with every competition. Without her, I wouldn't have been able to learn that not every day will be perfect, but that things would get better and I had to endure until they did. And without her, I wouldn't have been disciplined enough to push myself when every part of me wanted to stop. Training isn't easy, and training with your mom certainly isn't, and it took both of us a while to learn each of our limits.

While my mom helped to nurture the fighter in me in order to conquer my fears and become someone capable of winning the

Olympics, another person who helped me find ways to counter my "Olympic gold or bust" mentality was Shae. I was absolutely training to win gold, but after 2018 I was trying to put that pursuit in the broader context of realizing that if I didn't, it wouldn't be the end of the world, that it wouldn't define me. I was learning that the Olympics is not just a goal but a journey; and this time, I wanted to appreciate the road to getting there more. She taught me to shift my thinking to focus more on being grateful for the opportunity of competing at the Olympics, than on seeing the Games as a source of stress and dread, like in 2018. Yes, the Olympics brings a lot of pressure and expectation, but it's also an amazing experience I was fortunate enough to live through. Shae helped me to take time to look up at the lights in the arena, or to notice the color of the seats in the stadium, and to touch and feel the ice. She really pushed this mentality of being grateful rather than regretful and afraid. When I would feel down if things weren't going well during our choreography sessions or in practice, she was the one who helped me to take a breather—literally, with breathing exercises—and put all the frustration aside and remind myself how much I loved the feel of the ice under me and the flow of power that came from digging in with the edges of my skate blades.

I think focusing on gratitude helped to make the Beijing Olympics a drastically different experience from the PyeongChang Games. It was something that took me some time to learn, but I was getting more comfortable with this strategy with every passing year. In training for Beijing, I added another important person to my team, who addressed the major gap I still had in my preparation—working on my mental resilience.

I spent the majority of my skating career not appreciating, and maybe even dismissing, the importance of mental health for athletes. It's the area where I had to do the most growing. I had this bias that performing at the elite level was almost exclusively dependent on physical well-being, so it wasn't easy to shift my thinking. U.S. Figure Skating actually puts all its athletes in touch with a sports psychologist before every season, to do an assessment of where you are mentally and to identify any issues you might be having. I remember these evaluations started when I was pretty young, so at that time I never really understood that a sports psychologist could help with performance-related issues. The check-ins were kind of routine. I remember thinking that they were mostly about interpersonal relationships, and I didn't comprehend how they could benefit my skating.

I did this for the first few years after I started skating at international competitions, and then in 2017, I asked my mom to help find me a sports psychologist who didn't work with other figure skaters, since I had heard other elite athletes were using them. The psychologist talked to me about pre-competition nerves and asked if I had anxiety about competition. I explained that I did, but while I thought she was great, I didn't think such anxiety was unusual, so I remember seeing her only once.

Even as I was preparing for the 2018 Games, I didn't fully recognize the importance of having a sports psychologist's support in mentally preparing for an experience like the Olympics. I thought I knew myself better than any outsider ever could, so I decided that I would figure things out on my own. I had also felt this way because after speaking to a bunch of Olympic skaters, I wasn't able to connect their advice and experiences to much of my specific situation. I strongly believed that nobody could understand how I felt about the Olympics, or really conceptualize the pressure I was feeling and the daily frustrations of training, so I was just pushing through it all alone.

Admittedly, a lot of that was driven by inertia, too. Naturally I always felt the most pressure before competitions, but competitions flash by so quickly that I would experience this insane spike in adrenaline and pressure around the event. Then, right after I competed, all that anxiety immediately plummeted. In the heat of the moment, I needed every resource possible to get through the competition, but as soon as I was done, I would think, "I'm self-sufficient and I made it through, so I don't really need any additional help." That mentality might have also been a product of the fact that I started competing when I was so young, and never really struggled with issues of stress. In my mind, all that mattered was how I performed. For the longest time, I thought that had everything to do with how well I was physically prepared.

That attitude ultimately proved to be my downfall in 2018. I was wrong to expect navigating something as monumental and emotionally charged as the Olympics is a solo gig.

Even after 2018, I thought I could take care of my mental preparation by myself. I had heard from other athletes and read about mindfulness training, so I learned a few techniques on my own, including breathing exercises and ways to refocus my mind when I was feeling nervous. I used these before the World Championships in Stockholm in 2021, and I didn't feel better at all. So I knew I needed help. And I was finally ready to accept that help.

I decided that I needed to add a mental coach to my team before Beijing, because I didn't want to leave any stone unturned if I got a second chance to compete at the Olympics. But just as with my coach, finding the right person whom I felt comfortable with was critical.

It wasn't until the spring of 2021, just after the World Championships, that my agent, Yuki, found Dr. Eric Potterat, who works with the Los Angeles Dodgers as the director of their Specialized Performance Programs. Eric retired from the U.S. Navy after twenty years of service as a commander where he was the head psychologist for the Navy SEALs, and was the sports psychologist for the U.S. Women's National Soccer Team when they won the World Cup in 2019. Perhaps it was that military background, but after speaking with him, I really liked his structured and regimented approach. He had worked with the best competitors on the planet, Olympians, World Cup Champions, and had a World Series win; and the fit made sense for what I wanted to focus on. I've worked with him for almost a year now and I have yet to meet him in person because we've had all our sessions via Zoom or the phone.

In our first meeting, which was for around only twenty minutes, I explained to him what my goals were for the upcoming Olympic season, how I had felt in 2018, and that I wanted to overcome whatever mental hurdle had stood in my way then. I explained that mindfulness hadn't really helped me; and he said something to the effect that "If there's one thing I can guarantee, it's that by the time the Olympics rolls around, you will have zero doubt that you can perform well when you need to." That confidence was refreshing—I was immediately on board.

In our next meeting, Eric asked me questions about my history, and I was still trying to gauge if and how he could help me. He gave me a questionnaire that delved into what mental skills I already possessed and which skills I needed to improve on. The questions involved things like whether I had a program to manage stress in place before I competed, how I felt physically during training, how confident I felt during training, what my mindset was before getting on the ice, and how confident I felt when I competed. He also asked if I was good at visualizing, which I wasn't at the time, and whether I was adept at controlling my emotions—again, something I hadn't really been very successful in managing. He used the questions to build my personal profile and put structure around the mental techniques I used during practice and the ones I used during competition. The idea was to leverage the strengths and teach actionable ways to improve.

I really liked how matter-of-fact he was. I was looking for a mental training program that would set me up to manage the stress and pressure that I always felt at competitions. Eric provided just that. He was forward-thinking and had a precise plan for techniques that addressed my specific problems, like getting over my frustration when practices weren't going well or pulling myself out of the downward spiral of doom and gloom I tended to feel at competitions if I wasn't confident with all my elements. During our sessions, he presented his information on slides and gave me homework. It felt a lot like training for my mind, just like Brandon and Raf were training my body.

In fact, I saw a lot of similarities between the way Eric worked and the way Raf and Brandon worked, and I think that's why I found our discussions so productive. Aside from the start of every session, when he would ask me about how I was feeling about life in and out of training, or about any other issues that might be plaguing me at the time, the bulk of our discussion would be focused on specific tasks or techniques he wanted me to learn to become more mentally resilient. The goal was taking back control of my anxiety and not letting the pressure of competing overwhelm me.

After a few sessions with Eric, scattered throughout that summer before the Olympic season, I realized how little mental preparation I had had going into PyeongChang. I had never explored this aspect of readiness, and I had no idea what I was missing.

We never really had a regular schedule for sessions; we met mostly when I felt I needed to talk. He would message me every couple of weeks, asking if I was ready for another session and whether I had had any trouble applying the techniques he'd provided me. Over that summer, I worked on honing three skills that Eric introduced and that I relied on pretty heavily during the Olympics in Beijing.

The first was positive self-talk: finding the correct words that generate confidence. For every person these words are different. For me, it was reminding myself that every step I took and every mistake I made were part of a learning process. In the past, when I fell or popped a jump, I would tell myself, "I can't do this, I can't land this jump." I was using negative words, and that negativity would feed back and breed more frustration. I would end up losing confidence. Typically, on bad training days, I would fill my brain with thoughts like, "That jump was bad, or that spin was crap." Eric worked with me on using more positive words to pull me out of the negative spiral. If my jumps weren't going well, I would try to tell myself that my technique needed improvement, which then led me to thinking more critically about how I could adjust what I was doing to land the jump correctly.

The other aspect of positive self-talk was to flip the script, especially when I made a mistake, or was afraid of making a mistake, while I competed. Instead of dwelling on the potential for error, I trained myself to focus on all the times that I had landed a troublesome jump or skated a clean program. The key was to remind myself that if I had done it before, then I could do it again.

Related to this was another skill he emphasized: being in the right mindset. This involved focusing on being an athlete while I was on the ice, but recognizing that the intense drive and discipline I adopted there wasn't necessarily appropriate off the ice in my relationships with family and friends. Mindset is deeply tied to the roles you play. Your mindset should switch and adjust as the roles you play throughout your life, or even throughout the day, shift and change.

This was especially impactful for navigating the pressures I felt from the expectations I placed on myself before the Olympics. In 2018, I had shouldered those expectations from myself, my family, figure skating fans, and the public in an unhealthy way. I never stopped trying to be Nathan Chen, Olympic figure skater. I never gave myself a break from that mindset. And ultimately it became too much.

When I heard Simone Biles talk about this when she made the brave decision to withdraw from the Tokyo Olympics after all the expectations that had been placed on her, I felt a lot of empathy for what she was going through. She was experiencing pressure on a level I've never felt. Her comments about how the media and the public often see athletes as superhuman and somehow immune to the emotions and pressures other people feel were really relatable for me. I was happy that someone was talking about the things that I also felt but couldn't express. I was impressed that she was able to do that.

The conversation around mental health was changing. Hearing athletes like Simone speak about their struggles helped me realize that my work with Eric was something that was, and should be, as integral a part of preparing for something like the Olympics than I had ever given it credit for.

The last aspect, and one of the skills I used most frequently in Beijing, was visualization, which was a big part of Eric's strategy for me. I had tried visualization before, but every time I did, I couldn't help but see myself falling, making mistakes, popping jumps, or just doing the most tragic things. Eric really harped on spending extra time visualizing several times a day. He drilled into me how to visualize properly—down to granular details that would help to teach my mind how to guide my body on what to do. He suggested that I do these exercises at night, because you build memories when you sleep. Just before I fell asleep, he wanted me to see myself performing flawless programs so I would remember to execute them that way the next day.

At first, I wasn't really good at doing that, but I started to visualize throughout the day, whenever I could grab a few minutes—while brushing my teeth or taking some time for myself during a walk or on a break. He wanted me to get as detailed as possible, so I would not only visualize a jump but also try to resurrect the sound of the ice crunching under my blades, the way the air smelled, the feeling of the air in my mouth as I spun around, the feeling in my fingers, and even the sensation of the clothes on my body while I was turning in the air. It wasn't simply about the pure technique of the jump, but was a very sensation-based visualization so I could really embrace the whole experience of a perfect program and sear it into both my brain and my body. He felt that creating those mental connections would jump-start the same sensations and muscle memory when I needed them during a competition, even if my nerves or anxiety took over like they had in 2018.

Throughout my time in Beijing, I incorporated more visualization into my approach. Before I had practice on the main rink at Capital Indoor Stadium, I would stand off-ice there and map out where I would do my jumps and visualize myself doing those elements at the exact place where I needed to execute them. The more I saw myself doing that in my mind's eye, the more likely I would actually do them when I needed to. Every day before I competed, I would sit and think a bit about different elements every hour or so—I would go over a perfect quad Lutz a few times, or a quad Salchow or a triple Axel. They were brief exercises, but I did them pretty regularly whenever I was away from the rink.

Not everything about all the mental coaching strategies worked for me, though, especially for competitions that season leading up to the Olympics. For example, I found that breathing techniques to calm myself didn't really work for me right before I competed. I had tried them before my first Grand Prix event and didn't find them useful; in fact, the breathing exercises made me feel even more antsy. But they did help the night before an event, especially if I had trouble sleeping. For that, I relied on a few different apps, like Calm and Headspace, to guide me through those exercises.

Looking back, the resources for me to strengthen my mental approach to competing were always there, but I hadn't been ready to take advantage of them. When I was finally ready to use them, they helped me enormously.

8 TAKING A DIFFERENT APPROACH

条条大路通罗马

All roads lead to Rome.

Music is a critical part of my sport. Skating gives me a chance to play characters and express different aspects of my personality that I might not otherwise realize exist. And music is the gateway to doing that.

I've always had an affinity for music, maybe before I even remember. My first instrument was the toy piano I was transfixed by at the Toys R Us when I was a baby. When I was a toddler, my mom remembers me sitting at our upright piano one day and just banging on the keys. I must have been trying to emulate my sisters, who were taking lessons at the time, but I got really mad and threw a tantrum. When my mom asked me why I was so upset, I told her that I couldn't understand why the piano wasn't cooperating and wouldn't play "Jingle Bells." It was really my lack of ability that was the problem, but I took it out on our poor piano. My mom then thought it was time for some piano lessons.

I really enjoyed taking lessons, but like so many kids who pick up music early, I found practicing to be a chore. I remember my mom would leave my brother Colin and me at home to practice—the piano for me, the cello for Colin—while she went to the store. As soon as she left, we'd stop and do something else, keeping an eye on the window for her return. When we saw her car pull into the driveway, I sprinted to the piano and Colin back to his cello. We did have fun playing music together, though. Colin once had a cello recital and needed a piano accompaniment, so my mom asked me to do it; it was fun to play together.

I took lessons for about six years, and enjoyed learning new pieces. Those early years I took my playing quite seriously and I even competed in (and won) some local piano competitions. But as I started spending more time at the rink, my piano practice time became limited, so my playing became less serious, more as a hobby.

When I started traveling back and forth from Utah to California, my mom bought me an electronic keyboard so I could keep playing. But when I moved to California and I was twelve, we couldn't get an acoustic piano for me to practice on in our tiny cabin at Lake Arrowhead, so playing the piano took a back seat for a while. I missed playing on an acoustic instrument, so my mom thought a violin might be easier to travel with as I started going to more competitions in different states. Again, having watched my sisters play the violin, I thought I could pick it up as well. My mom drove me to a teacher about an hour from Lake Arrowhead to get violin lessons once a week. After I broke my hand in 2014, I couldn't practice violin anymore, so I gave that up pretty quickly.

I still wanted to play some kind of portable instrument, so I turned to the guitar, which Colin played. That turned out to be my favorite instrument, and I still play. The learning curve was pretty shallow, so I got hooked quickly when I started making progress and could strum some simple things. While the learning curve gets steeper as you learn more, I was able to learn a lot of songs online through YouTube. I never took formal lessons for any extended period of time, like I did with piano, and guitar's not something I practice regularly, but for me it's a fun and relaxing thing to do. Time can pass quickly when I'm playing; I can easily while away an hour on the guitar learning a new song.

Playing the guitar, especially at competitions, can keep my mind off skating. I turn to music around competition time, so whenever I have an event coming up, I tend to play a lot more. When I was at Yale, I ended up going back to the piano a decent amount. I'm pretty shy about playing when there are a lot of people around, but I would usually be in New Haven during spring break preparing for the World Championships. The week before I would leave to compete, campus would be completely empty and the music rooms were deserted. So I could play a lot more and I really enjoyed it.

A year before the Beijing Games, I got an electric guitar and began learning how to play songs on it. When I'm at competitions, I bring my guitar and play. I had it with me in Beijing, along with a baby amp, and jammed around with some Beatles songs to decompress.

For the 2021–2022 Olympic season, I asked Shae to choreograph both my short and free programs. For the short program, I told Shae that I wanted something like "Nemesis" from 2018. While I hadn't skated well in that program, I liked the energy and uniqueness of Benjamin Clementine's vocals and the melody. I generally don't like skating to pieces I know have been used many times before. I also need to feel a strong connection with the music. I was looking for something that conveyed a certain level of intensity and energy, since that's what I felt I needed at the Games.

She had pulled a bunch of pieces for me to listen to, but none of them really stood out. Since I liked "Nemesis," she suggested some other pieces by Clementine, but even those didn't seem right. None quite expressed the energy that I was looking for. One of his compositions, though, did sound very interesting to me—"Eternity." But it was slower and a little moodier than I wanted for a short program. Just for fun, we played "Nemesis" on the speakers at the rink for comparison, and immediately all my coaches perked their heads up. We felt its quicker beat and brighter piano and percussion were a better fit than the subtler "Eternity."

After thinking about it, Shae, Raf, and I decided to combine the two songs, starting out with "Eternity" and then picking up the pace to end with "Nemesis." I was of course thinking about the baggage that "Nemesis" brought—those two awful skates I had in PyeongChang—but I figured that by the time that song came on, I would be done with my big jumps and have only footwork left, so any negative thoughts wouldn't really be a concern. I really liked the program, and we planned out my jump layout: starting out with a quad Lutz, then a triple Axel, then in the second half of the program, a quad flip–triple toe combination. That last jumping pass would help me to collect those important bonus points.

For the free program, Shae and I went in a more classical direction, with a medley of pieces by Mozart, including the "Dies Irae" from his Requiem. I had wanted to skate to Mozart since I was a kid, but never found the right time to do so. This piece really worked for me, and I thought Shae did an incredible job of choreographing my elements so they followed the swells of the music.

In a normal season, I would generally test-drive my new programs at Japan Open in early October. But because of COVID-19, Japan Open organizers could not invite foreign skaters in 2021, and I had to debut both programs in late October at my first competition of the Olympic season and Grand Prix—2021 Skate America.

Skating programs in training and skating them in competition feel extremely different. As much fun as I had creating and training the two programs, when I competed at Skate America, I didn't feel engaged, especially in the short program. I fell on the quad Lutz, and I stumbled out of the quad flip and couldn't finish the combination with the triple toe. Somehow, when I competed that short program, I wasn't feeling the flow of the jumps. I wasn't necessarily thinking of 2018 because of the "Nemesis" part of the music, but it was more that I didn't feel connected to the program overall. My performance felt a little flat, and I didn't really have time to recover and rest between the jump and spin elements. Throughout the whole program, I felt as if I was trying to do a lot, but not a lot was actually getting done. I don't know if the program just had bad juju or not, but I didn't feel great competing it.

I actually liked the free program, although I also made some mistakes in that, doubling two of my quads. My Olympic teammate Vincent Zhou skated really well and won that competition, and I came in third behind Shoma Uno of Japan. I admit that I was not as well prepared as I could have been for that event, and it was a great wake-up call for me.

After I finished competing, my sisters and Orestes, who had come to watch me compete, joined my mom and me as we talked things out with them, because we wanted to make sure we were on the same page.

The five of us sat in Alice's hotel room, and we had one of the most important conversations before the Olympics. We talked about how I felt about this upcoming season, and how my mom could help me. My mom felt that I was not taking control of my responsibilities as an athlete and that my discipline was wavering. I agreed and spoke about how I planned to take on more responsibility and the different approaches that I could try. We discussed how much autonomy I should have and in what way my mom should be involved in my training. We defined our roles clearly to achieve the goals we wanted.

Having Alice and Janice there really helped, I think, to mediate some of the differences in my and my mom's philosophies that had emerged when we were in California. My sisters made sure that my mom and I wouldn't interrupt the other, and could fully express whatever it was we felt was being misunderstood or left unsaid. We finally agreed that I would need to be more accountable for my training, and that I would document my daily training plan so we could have discussions once a week to minimize the otherwise constant focus on skating. She would assist in the few weeks leading up to a competition, but would let me make the training decisions I needed to gain confidence.

After that conversation, I thought we needed clearer leadership and wanted to continue improving the communication within the team of my mom, Raf, and me, so I asked Raf to meet us at a café the next morning. To that point, we had only communicated indirectly, which I felt wasn't productive or useful. I wanted all of us to work as a team, as partners during the upcoming Olympic journey. I told them that I took responsibility for some of the less than mature and arrogant ways I had behaved, and in thinking that I could forge ahead on my own. I acknowledged that I was also not giving Raf the attention he deserved, and told him that my mom and I decided that it would be best for her not to come to the rink every day so Raf and I could get to work for three of the next five weeks before my next competition.

I asked Raf what he felt we needed to do. He said our work from the previous year, during the off-season when we focused on refining my jump technique, was really critical for my development, and that he wanted to bring that training back. I had been so focused on training just my programs that I wasn't appreciating his focus on the mechanics of my skating. We agreed that when I returned from my next competition, Skate Canada, which was the following weekend in October, we would follow his lead for three weeks, and after that we would return the focus on program run-throughs before the next competition, the Grand Prix Final in December. We also agreed that I would be the captain of the ship, and that each person had to voice what they thought I needed to help me stay accountable and on the right path to succeed for the remainder of that season.

Later, Raf told me that when I called that meeting, he knew that I'd have a successful season, because he saw my decision as a sign that I was finally taking ownership of my skating—the way he had always wanted me to since I started working with him.

My mom also agreed. Raf called her from time to time to update her on how my training was going. He even asked her to stop by the rink to see our progress, but she declined, knowing that we were on the right track and eager to have Raf continue to build on the work he and I were doing.

Skate America catalyzed the need to improve the inner workings of the team, but it also brought attention to something just as pressing.

After Skate America and my disappointing short program, I had asked Alice and Janice for feedback. Both of them wondered whether going back to "Nemesis," even for only a small part, was a good idea, given everything that I associated with it. I kind of agreed, so I decided that after Skate Canada I would tell Raf that I felt something was off, and that I wanted to change my program.

At first, Raf was hesitant. "We don't have time to switch to a completely new program right now," he said, which was absolutely true. But he also told me to think about what other programs I had done in the past that I could bring back. I mentioned "La Bohème," which I had competed in the 2019–2020 season that was cut short because of the pandemic. I really liked that program, which Shae had choreographed, and I had scored a personal best with it at the 2019 Grand Prix Final. But I never competed that program at 2020 Worlds because they were canceled due to COVID-19. Raf was understanding and said, "The decision is yours. Truthfully, you just need to do your job, and your job is to land your jumps, to skate a clean program, and to perform. If you can find a piece of music you enjoy performing to, then it really doesn't matter; stick to something that you enjoy." He later confessed that he had hoped I would skate to Charles Aznavour again, since Aznavour, like him, was Armenian, and he was so excited I made this decision.

After Skate America, I provisionally decided to switch to "La Bohème" for my short program, and stick with the Mozart piece for my free for the season. However, I had only a couple of days before competing at Skate Canada so I ended up skating "Eternity" and the Mozart there, and won that event. I skated better than I had at Skate America, especially in the short program, but I was still feeling iffy about my short, which solidified my decision to switch.

Throughout my career, I have created great relationships with some of the officials at U.S. Figure Skating. One in particular, Tina Lundgren, has been my go-to person for feedback on my programs as they progress through the season. When I got back from Skate Canada, she and I got on a Zoom call so I could get her perspective as well as that of other judges and officials she had consulted on my new programs, especially since I had competed them two weeks in a row. I wanted to hear her thoughts on where to clean things up or be more precise in order to earn additional points on the program components score. On that Zoom, her mood was serious, and at first, I wasn't quite sure why. I hadn't told anyone about switching my short program yet, so I was a little nervous about what she was going to say.

"Well, I have some thoughts that might not be easy to hear," Tina started.

I jumped in and asked, "Is it my short program? Because I agree."

"No," she said. "Actually the feedback on the short program was pretty good. It's the free."

It turns out most of the officials didn't love the Mozart piece—they felt it wasn't as memorable as some of my previous free programs. Her concern was that the program didn't build enough energy until the very end, and that it wasn't having the impact on the officials that I would want from an Olympic program. Bottom line—she didn't think it was the right program to take to Beijing.

I was surprised. It was not the feedback I expected to hear at that point in the season, just two months before the U.S. National Championships—one of the most important competitions to qualify for the Olympics.

I was also frustrated because I had skated the "Eternity" and Mozart programs at Champs Camp before the season started and didn't get negative feedback then. But I was reminded that performing programs in practice or at a camp, even if it simulates a competition, isn't the same as seeing a program skated during a real live competition.

As surprised as I was about the reaction to the Mozart program, I was even more surprised when she suggested that I replace it with *Rocketman*. She explained how unique that program was and how it conveyed a lot of vitality and energy. She made the point that even if I didn't hit all of my jumps, *Rocketman* was a piece of music that would carry me through and create energy. The program built throughout and ended with an intense footwork sequence that was unique to me. It was more likely to pack a punch with the judges and any audience in attendance and make up for what was probably going to be a near empty arena because of Covid protocols. The Mozart program, on the other hand, was constructed with more of a steady pace, so if I missed jumps in between, the whole program could start to fizzle.

Tina ended by saying that she would support me regardless of my decision. If I stuck with Mozart she had three pages of notes prepared, but first I had to talk to everyone on my team and decide what I was going to do. Since she and I had worked together like this before, I took her suggestions seriously and went back to my team to discuss.

As disruptive as it was to think about changing both of my programs with so little time before Nationals, a part of me felt a little relieved. *Rocketman* was from the same season as "La Bohème," so I also never got to compete that program at the World Championships because of the pandemic.

I talked to Shae first, since she had choreographed both the "Eternity" and Mozart programs. She told me I had to make my own decision; I should think about the judging panel's input, but the decision had to be mine, not theirs. I knew she was right. I had been the one who worked with her, experimenting and learning and growing by putting the two programs together—and the Mozart program really did represent a different side of me. It showcased more maturity and depth in my skating. Shae supported whatever decision I made, but also pointed out that if I went back to a previous program, it would be a little like stagnating creatively.

I understood and appreciated what she was saying, but at the same time, realistically, one important aspect to building programs is to score well with the judges. I wasn't judging them; they were judging me. The officials who were trained to score programs were telling me that the Mozart program probably wouldn't be as well received.

It was a tough decision. I didn't want to hurt anyone's feelings. If I didn't skate to Mozart, I knew it might be a little disappointing to Shae. But if I kept Mozart, then maybe I would be performing a program that the judges wouldn't appreciate as much as *Rocketman*, which wouldn't help me in the end. On the other hand, Marie, who had choreographed *Rocketman*, was in Montreal, and I didn't have the time, nor did I want to travel there and risk getting COVID-19, to tweak that free program while Shae was right in Irvine and could keep refining the Mozart program over the coming weeks.

I consulted Raf, and he suggested listening to the *Rocketman* music again. "If it sounds old, or sounds like a dated program, then we keep Mozart," he said. "But if you listen to it and feel that it's still interesting and fun to skate to, then consider it."

We played it at the rink, and I skated through some of the choreography that I remembered. And I actually felt the music sounded fresh, very energetic, new, and youthful. I called up Tina again and told her that if she really felt switching to *Rocketman* was the right decision, then I was on board with it. There was an enthusiastic "Yesssss" on the other end of the phone. I also told her I wanted to change my short program as well and go back to "La Bohème."

Once I made the switch and started skating to the new-old programs again, everything seemed to click. The programs felt organic, and relearning them gave me a new motivation and excitement that carried me through the second half of the season. We didn't have much time left, which was a little nerve-wracking, but I was inspired by the challenge.

Vera Wang had designed costumes for my two previous programs, and when I told her I was going back to "La Bohème" and *Rocketman*, she thought I should have something fresh for the upcoming competitions rather than the outfits I had worn in 2019. Despite the time crunch, she was willing to come up with new designs. For "La Bohème," I wanted something more formal: a suit. Vera thought other competitors might be wearing suits, and that the look wouldn't be unique, but came up with the idea of keeping with the sleek style she normally designed for me but adding a faux lapel, which was challenging to make work. But she found the right fabric and construction and designed a costume that fit well with the mood of the Aznavour piece and allowed me to be comfortable in performing all my jumps. For *Rocketman*, she continued with the original theme of bright colors and created many designs. We then narrowed the options down to the ones we both liked. One was an orange and black background with a bright green rocket flare, reminiscent of Jupiter's great red spot, as the focal point, which I ended up wearing at U.S. Nationals. I wanted something a little more subdued for the Olympics, however, so she also designed an orange and yellow costume with a galaxy theme that I wore in Beijing.

I was really excited to perform the programs at the Grand Prix Final, scheduled for December 2021 in Osaka, but that event was canceled because of COVID-19. I had been counting on skating before a panel of international judges, similar to those who would be judging in Beijing, since it would give me an idea of what my scores might be. Without the Grand Prix Final, my only opportunity to skate those programs before the Beijing Olympics would be at the U.S. Nationals in January, 2022.

It's important to mention here that while my dad hadn't spent every day at the rink as my mom had, he was my armchair expert. By that I mean if I had concerns about what jump layout I should follow, he was the one I went to for the hard data on which option I should follow. He would calculate the technical points I could collect depending on the jump layouts I chose. I would send him ten different jump layouts and ask him to figure out the value of each, and then what my overall technical score might be, assuming an average grade of execution (GOE) score from the judges. Then I would ask him to calculate my potential technical score if the judges gave me perfect

GOE marks. We would compare these against scores my competitors had earned in past competitions, and also calculate scores for my competitors based on elements we thought they might perform. This helped me to figure out how technically difficult a program I needed to perform to come out on top. Between me, my mom, my dad, and Raf, we came up with what we knew was the right jump layout that I would need against my competitors in Beijing.

Once we were satisfied with the general jump layout, in the few remaining weeks before the competition, Shae worked with me on refining "La Bohème," and making slight adjustments to accommodate the new jump layouts I had planned. But working with Marie was trickier. I did a Zoom session with her, setting up my iPad at the rink, then having her watch as I skated through the free program in which I also had to make tweaks to include the different jump layout that I was training that season compared with the last time I skated that program. But the remote thing wasn't ideal, and I asked Marie if it would be okay to have someone else put the finishing touches on the program. She was completely understanding and said yes.

When I was training with Marina Zoueva in 2016, I had worked with another coach on her team, Massimo Scali, who was a former ice dancer. I had learned that he had been working in Northern California and was available to work with me, so in November of 2021 I asked him if he would be up for a very intense last-minute choreography tweak. He was gracious and made time for me, and we ended up changing the jump layout and adjusted the transitions of the program from how they had been laid out before by Marie. The cancellation of the Grand Prix Final ultimately was a blessing, since it gave us more time to work on really bringing out the character in the program, polishing my hand and arm movements, and finding ways to have fun with the music. For the first week Massimo was at the rink, I didn't even practice jumps—we just concentrated on all those other elements.

As I was skating through both "La Bohème" and *Rocketman*, I thought to myself, "These are really, really great programs." I hadn't had the same enjoyment earlier in the season, so I was feeling good that I had made the right decision.

And Tina was right—*Rocketman* definitely had more energy than Mozart, something I was reminded of quickly because I was getting exhausted running through the choreography. In Mozart, Shae and I had meticulously planned out the program so I could be efficient with my energy. With *Rocketman*, it was almost all high-intensity skating, so I was beat just a third of the way through. That's where Massimo was a huge help; he created more breathing points in the program, and I just had to condition and train harder to make sure I remained engaged throughout the entire four minutes and ten seconds of the program.

I was also experimenting with new ways to build up my stamina and—finally—train both harder and smarter.

My mom had drilled into me that practice makes perfect: the practice I put in beforehand would get me through, just as my training made it possible for me to skate that six-quad free program in PyeongChang. I had faith in her training philosophy, but this year I found a way to maintain that without tiring myself out. After two years at Yale, and finally adapting to Brandon's advice to be more flexible about my training volume, I had shifted my thinking about how I spent my time on the ice and found a way to make it more efficient. I don't know if I would have changed my perspective on this if I hadn't gone to college and been forced to make do with more limited ice time and training time.

While at college, with frequent exams and papers due, I had to skip some practices or cut them short to make sure I could complete my schoolwork. All that time I spent working through problem sets, reading class material, or preparing upcoming exams, was extra time I gave for my body to rest. In the end, that served as the dial that Brandon had always wanted me to use in adjusting the intensity of my training. Without really thinking about it, I had scheduled in lower-load skating days, when I had to study and during which I could rest and recover. It helped me realize the flip side of elite athletics: the need to prioritize rest and recovery as much as training.

The entire time I was at Yale, I didn't experience any serious injuries. Even my hip didn't bother me that much. That's because I wasn't constantly pounding on it with the really aggressive training that I was used to. I never needed any PRP injections. I also didn't have the intensive physical therapy I used to get but still wasn't in a lot of pain.

Through experimentation, Brandon and I came up with a threshold below which I could train without pain, and beyond which it would start to hurt again. So instead of taking the all-or-nothing approach of pushing myself to the breaking point and then being forced to take time off to recover that I had relied on in preparing for the 2018 Olympics, I devised a system of maintaining a steadier pace of jumps and decreasing that a bit leading into a competition so I would be at my peak for the competition. It turned out that doing about one hundred to a hundred twenty jumps on hard days and dialing that down to about sixty or so on lighter days would put me in a good place. Eventually, I developed a second sense for coming close to but not crossing this bar. If I compared the total number of jumps I did leading up to PyeongChang and the number I did training for Beijing, it was a bit less than before PyeongChang—except this time around, I made each attempt more precise, had a higher success rate, and gained confidence from each attempt.

Brandon didn't tell me until afterward, but the entire time I was in Beijing, he kept track of every jump I did from the day I arrived to the last jump of my free skate. He came to every practice, and manually ticked off not only how many jumps I did but which types of jumps. It turned out that I kept a pretty consistent pace of building from about sixty jumps up to eighty or so, then decreasing that number to the mid-forties the day before the team short and maintaining that until the individual short program.

Even with all this careful control, my right groin injury flared up really badly just two days before I left for Nationals. It was the most pain I'd felt with this injury in my entire skating career. Walking was painful, and jogging was out of the question. I seriously wondered how I would make it through the jumps I needed to do.

Whenever this groin pain had happened in the past, I knew that giving my hips a couple of days of rest would calm things down, so I only did light skating in the days before leaving for Nationals, which were in Nashville, Tennessee. When I arrived at the competition, my first practice was pretty good; I did a full free program and didn't feel too much pain.

The second day was a different story.

The pain was so bad that I couldn't tap my foot into the ice for flip or Lutz, and kicking my leg through for Axel was excruciating. When I got off the ice, took off my skates, and tried to stand up, I could barely walk. I thought, "I'm going to have to withdraw from Nationals." But if I didn't compete, the first time I would skate my new programs that season would be at the Olympics, and that wasn't ideal.

Three days before my competition, Brandon contacted the physical therapist at U.S. Figure Skating, Lauren Farrell, who was in Nashville, and asked her to help me. I told Lauren that I wanted to work with her every day during Nationals to manage my hip injury and get me through the competition. Other than rest, the best thing for the injury was to do exercises that would improve my range of motion and stabilize my core, because when my hip pain flared up, I would again compensate by using my adductors and hip flexors and end up straining them as well. Lauren worked with me to strengthen my glutes and core. I took a ton of Tylenol and Advil to get me through the practices. I was less worried about my programs at that point, and more anxious about whether, by competing, I would do more damage to my hip that would make me weaker or unable to compete at the Olympics if I qualified.

I substantially reduced the volume of jumps I tried during a couple of practices, and I even skipped one practice. Instead, I went to the rink and worked on stability exercises to strengthen my hip and prevent me from overcompensating with my other muscles. I attempted only the bare minimum of jumps. I would start with a triple, then try one of each quad type; the flip and Lutz were really painful.

I ended up adjusting my jump technique on the flip and Lutz a little bit to reduce the pressure on my hip. I also lowered the amount of force I used on that takeoff, which meant I needed to maximize my torque to get the rotations I needed without having as much height.

Adrenaline really pulled me through those programs, because, to be honest, they were a blur. After the free program, I could barely move. I told the U.S. Figure Skating officials I would have to skip the exhibition. I didn't want to make a big deal out of my injury and tried to limit the number of people who knew about it.

My injury wasn't the only thing occupying my mind that week. I was also particularly nervous about COVID-19 at Nationals— more than I had been at other competitions I had attended during the pandemic. A lot of things were adding up to make the situation kind of risky. There had been a huge outbreak at our rink, and many athletes were getting infected. Plus, people could buy tickets to the event, so we weren't in a bubble. And the official hotel where most skaters and officials stayed also had other guests not related to the competition. The closer we got to the Olympics, the more worried I was about testing positive and being ineligible to compete in Beijing. And with Nationals just a month before the Olympics, if I tested positive at Nationals, or in the weeks afterward, then I was worried it would take me weeks to recover and test negative again, which could put me in danger of not being able to compete at the Games. I was really concerned about how I would get through the event without getting COVID-19.

I probably made a pest of myself, talking to the team doctors about what would happen if we tested positive. And they weren't exactly reassuring. I had two worries: first, if I tested positive, then I wouldn't be able to compete and I didn't know how sick I would get and how much training I would miss. Second, I didn't know how long it would take until I would test negative again. I knew the Beijing Olympic officials required two negative tests in order for athletes to even fly to China. The team doctors told me that most people who were infected could clear the virus in about three to four weeks, but sometimes it took as long as eight to nine weeks to test negative.

"You realize that eight to nine weeks from now is basically the end of the Olympics?" I asked. "Is this a risk we should all be willing to take?"

But we really didn't have a choice, because Nationals was the final competition before the Olympics, and even though I could petition for a spot on the team if I couldn't compete at Nationals, I also wanted to have the experience of skating my programs before the Games. I had briefly thought about not going to Nationals. But since I hadn't competed at the Grand Prix Final because it was canceled, and had new programs I needed to try out, I decided to take the risk. I would just take every single precaution I could to protect myself.

I double masked with an N95 and a surgical mask the entire time I was in Nashville, beginning with the flight from California. I didn't stay in the official hotel where many of the competitors stayed. Instead my mom and I stayed at an Airbnb and she really went to extremes to keep a clean environment. As soon as I got back from practices or competing at the arena, she washed all my clothes and kept my gear by the door. It might have been overkill, but it was exactly what I needed to get through that competition, both mentally and practically. As it turned out, at least half a dozen athletes tested positive in Nashville, including 2022 world champion pairs skater Brandon Frazier from my rink and 2019 and 2020 national champion, Alysa Liu. Brandon and Alysa both petitioned successfully to make the Olympic team, based on their standings throughout the season.

Still, it was concerning. I felt that some of the testing policies should have been stricter. I had done a lot of reading about how the virus works, and talked to Janice as well, who helped me understand more about the virus and its incubation period. I'm not an epidemiologist or a health expert, but I thought we should have been tested every day at the competition. We were initially only tested before we left and tested again as soon as we arrived. But I worried that if anyone was infected during travel, it would have taken a few days to test positive. If we weren't tested daily, then there was the potential that some people who were positive but didn't know it were competing and possibly infecting others. That was really worrying, given how easily the Omicron variant spread.

I felt strongly enough about this that I spoke to U.S. Figure Skating officials and laid out my argument for daily testing. Part of my reasoning had to do with Beijing. Up to that point, at Grand Prix events, we were only tested before we left, then once we arrived, and not again until we left. But I knew the Beijing Olympic policies required daily testing, and we weren't prepared for that. It's not fun to have a swab stuck up your nose, but I think most athletes were okay with it, given the risk of infection that close to the Olympics. I also spoke to Rachel Flatt, the chair of the Athletes' Advisory Council at U.S. Figure Skating. She and the U.S. Figure Skating officials said they would consider it, and they ended up agreeing and started testing athletes and their support staff every day for the rest of the competition.

Despite all that, I was happy that I skated as well as I did, aside from the fact that I got so excited during the footwork in my free program to *Rocketman* that I tripped and fell on my stomach! Still, I was thrilled to earn my sixth national title, and, more importantly, guarantee my spot on my second Olympic team.

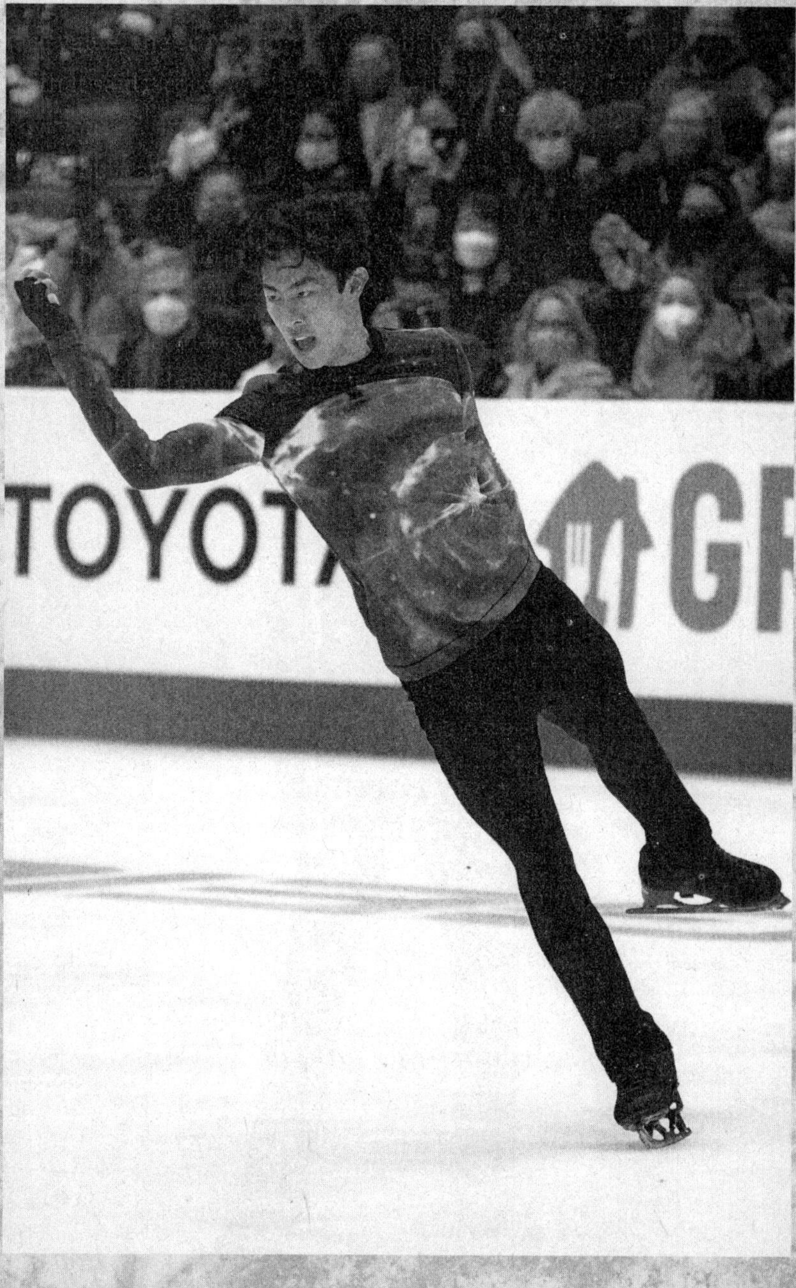

9 A SECOND CHANCE

有志者事竟成

Where there's a will, there's a way.

Once I got home from Nationals, the most immediate issue was addressing my hip. Brandon Siakel and my sports medicine team talked about my options for Beijing. I could get the PRP injections, which I hadn't received since the last Olympics. But that would mean four or five days of recovery, during which I could do only a very limited amount of skating. And I wanted to get the injections only from Dr. Philippon, in Vail, so it would mean my getting on a plane and risking COVID-19.

I could also try glucocorticoid injections, but the World Anti-Doping Agency (WADA) had banned its use in competition that January. I could apply for a therapeutic use exemption (TUE) to be permitted to use the glucocorticoid injections, but that was a lengthy and involved process.

Still, I asked Brandon to start the process of getting a TUE, as a backup plan, since, if approved, I could get the injection a day or two before I competed if I needed it. In the meantime, I decided to rely on manual therapy, similar to what I had gotten at Nationals, and on being more vigilant about trimming back the volume of training even more over the next three weeks. I got back on the ice as soon as I returned home from Nationals but didn't jump for a week. That's not exactly reassuring so close to the Olympics, but I had no choice. I would feel pain even doing crossovers, so I didn't want to push myself to the point where I couldn't compete in Beijing. Lauren had flown to California after Nationals to help me with recovery and to stabilize all the muscles surrounding my hip—my psoas, quadriceps, glutes, hip flexors, adductors, hamstrings, and lower back. She was trying to build up my glutes so that I could activate them more, which would stabilize my hip better and hopefully lead to less pain when I dug my toe pick into the ice to jump, or kicked through for that internal rotation on the Axel.

I was worried, of course, but I kept reminding myself that muscle issues like this one tend to resolve fairly quickly. It was just that when they flared up, it was really rough. And this time it was a lot worse than I had ever experienced before, so I didn't know how long it would take to recover.

Then one of those fluke accidents happened. After skating but not jumping for a week, my hip was feeling much better and I was ready to start trying my triples and quads. That morning, it had rained and I was warming up outside by running up and down the stairs on the side of the Great Park Ice building. As I turned to run down the stairs, my mom yelled, "Be careful!" Sure enough, I stepped on the corner of one of the slick steps and next thing I knew, I tumbled down and smacked the outside of my shin hard. I felt okay in that moment, but by the time I had to put on my skates, my foot hurt so much that I couldn't tie my laces. I was so frustrated because I had been looking forward to jumping again. It meant a few more days of no jumping, until the swelling went down, which actually turned out to be a blessing because it also gave my hip more time to heal. A few days later, my hip was feeling even stronger, my ankle swelling had gone down, and I was ready to start my final stretch of training to the Olympics.

The Olympics were looming large over the rest of January. The combination of performance-related and COVID-19-related worries made it hard for me to sleep. I had nightmares about testing positive and not being able to skate in Beijing. I was being as careful as I could, and constantly talked with the skating director at our rink, the doctors at U.S. Figure Skating, and with my mom about any interactions I had with people and whether I could do more to protect myself. I asked them what my risk was if I skated immediately after people left the ice, and whether I should wait a certain period of time before entering the ice after them. The threat of testing positive so close to the Olympics was stressful. Had I not had my team supporting me and reassuring me during those weeks, I definitely would have lost it. I leaned on Eric to figure out ways to manage these anxieties. He reminded me that as long as I was doing everything I could to protect myself, whether or not I got COVID-19 was really out of my control and not something I should spend my energy worrying about.

Our skating manager at Great Park Ice, Jacqui Palmore, worked really hard to mitigate the risk for the skaters training there. She convinced management to give the Olympic athletes as much private ice time as possible and scheduled me at different rinks in the Great Park facility to reduce my potential exposure to COVID-19. She brought an industrial aerosol sanitizer and sprayed the rink and provided loads of Lysol and wiped every surface we might come in contact with. She parked herself at the door to the rink while I trained to prevent anyone other than my immediate team from entering. The hockey players who trained there feared her strict enforcement of adherence to COVID-19 measures, and reflexively reached for their masks whenever they came near the entrance to the ice sheet. She even escorted me in and out of the rink and stood by while I put on and took off my skates to make sure I wasn't approached by anyone. Thanks to her, the Great Park management team, and Mitch Moyer at U.S. Figure Skating, I had three hours of private ice time every day to train in those weeks before Beijing. I am truly grateful for having had such dedicated ice time, and I am so grateful to Jacqui and the Great Park team for giving me that opportunity. I don't know if I could have avoided getting COVID-19 in that time if not for Jacqui's, the rink management's, and my mom's vigilance.

Aside from worrying about catching COVID-19, my other nightmares naturally had to do with competing. I had two kinds of dreams. In one, I skated really well and I won, which made me feel both good and a little anxious—since when I woke up, I realized it was a dream and I still had to go train to make it a reality. The other dream was pretty much a replay of 2018. I was worried about the quadruple Lutz–triple toe in the short program, my last and riskiest jump, so I dreamed that I missed it. I dreamed I missed a bunch of jumps and everyone else skated really well. I would then watch my name drop and drop in the rankings, just as I had after the free program in PyeongChang.

To enhance my chances of skating as well as I could in Beijing, I arranged to have Massimo come back to Great Park to work with me in the month before the Olympics. Nearly every day, he and I would work for three one-hour sessions, cleaning up my program. In the first session, I would warm up my jumps and do some of the jump sets that Raf had asked me to practice. Then Massimo would focus on my footwork and the details of my body placement at the end of the session. During the second session, I would focus on the short program, and my goal was to complete three clean short programs during the session. Because I struggled on the quad Lutz–triple toe combination in the second half of the program, I would try to land this combination cleanly three times a day as well. Finally, in the third session I concentrated on my free program, really drilling into the footwork sequence in the middle of the program. He wanted to see sharp arm movements from me and cleanly skated turns so nothing would distract from the constant forward momentum and high energy of the program. My goal was to execute a clean free program every day. Some days in order to do that, I would skate multiple free programs in a session.

After that, I would turn my attention to the second half of the program, as Raf wanted me to do. Raf would come to watch every session but didn't say too much to interrupt my work with Massimo unless he saw something that really needed correcting. With this routine, my confidence started to build. Unlike in 2018, I was able to skate strong programs in training.

In some ways, as ominous and disruptive as COVID-19 was, it served as a distraction from focusing on skating and all the expectations that I felt around the Olympics. This time, I was really trying to focus on what I wanted from the Games and what I could control, rather than getting pulled into feeling responsible for what others expected, as I had before the last Olympics. In some sense, for all of us who competed in Beijing, COVID-19 brought us closer together because it was something we shared, a challenge we all needed to manage—with masks, testing, and social distancing.

At Nationals, we had a meeting with U.S. Figure Skating officials about the upcoming Olympics. They went over the COVID-19 requirements for anyone traveling to Beijing. For these Olympics, the Beijing Olympic Committee was requesting that anyone coming to China for the Games—athletes, coaches, and staff—fly in on approved charter flights, to minimize the risk of introducing COVID-19 to the country. Additionally, no overseas spectators, including athletes' families, would be allowed to attend. Essentially, the goal was to initiate the COVID-19 bubble with the flight. The USOPC was providing flights from a few U.S. cities, including Los

Angeles, which was good for me since I didn't have to travel else-where to catch that plane.

We also had to provide two negative PCR tests, ninety-six and seventy-two hours before we boarded our flights; and the second test had to be from a lab that was approved by the Beijing government. Thankfully the USOPC worked with local Chinese consulates to make sure everyone was able to get tested at the right locations, but that added an extra layer of logistics to the process. Every person going to the Games had to provide proof of vaccination. We also had to provide daily health status updates on an app beginning four-teen days before our flight, including taking our temperatures and answering an online questionnaire about any COVID-19 symptoms like fever, cough, or sore throat. The whole process was thorough, which I appreciated.

Navigating all that kept me occupied so I didn't have much time to sit at home and worry about skating. Every day was a new logis-tical hurdle to make sure I completed all of the COVID tests, that I watched all of the orientation videos, and that all of my paperwork was in order. The goal was to receive a green health code on your health app that would be your authorization to boarding the flight for Beijing.

We were scheduled to leave from Los Angeles on January 27, but the USOPC wanted us to get to LA a week before the flight so we could go through team processing and COVID-19 testing at a local hotel. We needed to register and get our credentials, which are the key to getting into the Olympic Village and the arena in Beijing, and pick up all our Team USA gear. It's always exciting to see the opening and closing ceremony outfits, as well as the clothes that we would es-sentially be living in for the next three weeks or so. You really start to feel as if you're part of a team when you see the letters U-S-A.

Being with the members of Team USA who came from other cities, while great, was also stressing me out. I had felt safe from COVID-19 at home for three weeks after Nationals, but suddenly being forced to be around so many people, even though I knew they had been tested and were taking precautions just like I was, still made me anxious. Since I lived in Southern California, I was permitted to bypass the week-long stay at the hotel, and instead come in for the seventy-two-hour Chinese consulate–approved PCR test, and get sized for my gear and head back home. However, I was required to spend the night before the flight in the hotel. The hotel was semi-blocked for us, but there were guests not with the Team USA delegation also staying there. By that point, every single decision I had made was to minimize my chances of getting COVID-19, and I didn't want to risk everything at the last minute. Although I had checked in to the hotel that night, I became so worried that I called my mom and asked her to pick me up and take me home for the night; we came back the next morning to join the team.

I felt much better about the flight, because the only people on the plane were the first cohort of athletes, coaches, or Olympic staff, all of whom were vaccinated and tested. Janice kept reminding me that masks were my best defense against the virus, so I wore my glasses, an N95 mask, a KF94 on top of that, and a face shield. I decided I would rather look silly than not do it and get COVID-19. I figured that if I ended up getting COVID-19 after all that, then it was just meant to be.

I was kind of surprised that so many on that flight seemed more relaxed about things. They were mingling, and some people even had their masks under their noses, which made me wish everyone would get back to their seats.

I decided that I wasn't going to eat or drink anything on that flight so I wouldn't have to take my masks off. I chugged a bunch of water before I got on the plane to get hydrated, and didn't drink or eat anything for the entire fourteen-hour flight to Seoul, where the plane refueled although we didn't disembark.

I intentionally didn't sleep much the night before the flight because I wanted to start getting used to the time zone difference. That worked well, and I slept most of the first part of the flight. When I was awake, I watched some Marvel movies and read a book Janice had given me called *Dataclysm*.

When we finally landed, I was (of course) starving, but we still had a lot of testing and processing to go through. We were tested again at the airport—the first of many swabs that I would get over the next couple of weeks—and then we picked up our bags and headed to the Village. Once we were in our rooms, we couldn't leave until the results from our airport tests were negative.

To my relief, I didn't get any flashbacks from being back at the Olympics again. As soon as we got to the Village and walked through the plaza with all the flags from participating countries, I just felt excited.

The USOPC brought some freeze-dried meals for us in case we wanted specific types of foods, so I grabbed a pad Thai to heat up in the microwave in our suite since we couldn't leave our rooms for a while. I shared the space with other skaters, including Brandon Frazier, Evan Bates, and Jean-Luc Baker. Before I ate, I thoroughly cleaned my room and sanitized everything with wipes I had packed. I even sanitized all my bags and left my shoes outside the door.

I don't bring a whole lot of personal things with me when I compete, and I didn't want to feel that this experience was any different from any other competition. I brought my guitar and a baby amp to help me relax, and besides competition neccesities, this was about it when it came to personal items.

The U.S. security officials were also concerned about our digital security, and the USOPC had advised everyone not to bring their own phones or computers, so U.S. Figure Skating provided us with iPhone 8 rentals to take into China. I rely on my phone a lot, so I knew that it would be important for me to be able to contact my team—my family, Raf, Brandon, and Eric. I scroll through social media constantly, but it wasn't recommended that I log in to my accounts to access my normal content on the new phone, so I ended up using YouTube to find some of my favorite channels, like Hodinkee and cooking videos, to watch before going to bed. I also need my music and my videos—I need my program music so I can do run-throughs of them off the ice, and I'm always listening to or watching something as white noise both during the day and just before I fall asleep, so it's important for me to have access to my favorites. I ended up playing episodes of *Parks and Recreation* from YouTube to fall asleep to.

Normally, I spend a lot of time on Instagram, but not seeing my feed at all while I was there was actually kind of clutch. Besides YouTube, I was able to access Twitter, but I used it only to follow Jackie Wong—a figure skating analyst—to keep updated on how the competitions were going. It was nice not to be constantly bombarded by what major sports outlets were posting, or what my friends were posting, or what my competitors were posting. Staying off social media helped me to be more present and focused on what I needed to do.

I slept really well that night, and for the rest of the time I was in Beijing. When I woke up the next morning, the first thing I did was check my test result. Fortunately, it was negative.

Since it was evening back home in LA, I FaceTimed my mom and showed her all my Team USA gear. Throughout my time in Beijing, I FaceTimed my sisters a lot and showed them my room and various sites around the Village, including the dining hall. Alice remembers I called her, raving about the fruit they served, which was really good. I think that helped to keep me focused on what I had to do without getting overly stressed about being at the Games. My second Olympic experience had begun.

The team event was scheduled to start the day of Opening Ceremonies. U.S. Figure Skating makes decisions about which skaters will compete in each portion of the competition, taking into account requests from the athletes. And just as I had in 2018, I indicated to U.S. Figure Skating that my preference would be to skate in the team men's short program, because that would give me an extra chance to get on Olympic ice and allow me enough time to train before the men's individual event began.

I was of course feeling nervous about the team event; but this time, instead of simply hoping that things would go right, I actually had tools to ensure that they would.

Leading up to Beijing, Eric and I worked on making sure I could use them whenever doubts appeared. An important one was focusing on gratitude. I reminded myself that I was at the Olympics and how thankful I was for having the opportunity to compete. Rather than seeing the short program as a hurdle, I flipped it around and thought of it as a chance—a chance to take control. Eric helped me to realize that if I'm afraid of making a mistake, I probably will make that mistake. So if I knew something bad could happen, I just needed to do something to make it not happen. If I could skate poorly, I could also skate really well: it was all a matter of how I directed my thoughts. That was a helpful trick for me—the idea that my body will follow my thoughts. Even in a stressful situation, if I forced myself to smile and think happy thoughts, then my body would follow and I will feel happier. Most of all, Eric reminded me to have fun, texting me "have FUN" in caps.

Having Eric as part of my team made a big difference for me

in Beijing. I ended up texting him a few times a week, whenever I started to feel overwhelmed. Since the team event was one of the first events at the Olympics, I got to Beijing several days early. Each skater is assigned to a practice group with others in the men's competition. In those first couple of days there were maybe two people on the ice during my session, and we could play our music as often as we wanted. Once more people arrived we only got one chance during our practice to play our music during the official practice sessions.

I approached those early training sessions as genuine home practice sessions. We got to skate not only on the practice rink but also on the main rink, where we would be competing. I ended up running through my short program on the competition rink three times a day, like I had been doing back home. And while they weren't perfect, having those extra repetitions on official Olympic ice served as a game changer. It allowed me to get super comfortable with the ice, super comfortable with my skating patterns, and super comfortable with just being in that environment several times without having all the eyes watching me. It felt very peaceful.

But as more media started arriving and attending practices, I started feeling more pressure—I would think about their expectations, and everyone else's, and they began weighing on me. I texted Eric for help, telling him that I was starting to feel as though I had to perform well, and that worry was leaching into my practices. I was also getting increasingly worried about COVID-19 as more people began testing positive upon arrival. I wore a mask the entire time I was in Beijing: during every practice; when I was alone in my room; and, yes, even while I slept. I wasn't taking any chances.

But, no matter how careful you are, there was no escaping COVID-19, and it hit really close to home for Team USA. My teammate Vincent Zhou, who skated in the free program of the team event, tested positive the following day and had to withdraw from the men's individual event. It was heartbreaking, and I felt for him because I knew how hard he had trained and how careful he had been to protect himself from COVID-19.

To alleviate my growing anxiety about the Olympics and COVID-19, Eric told me that I should be focusing on only the things I could control. When I had trouble with my Lutz jump, he reminded me that since I didn't have additional training time, the only thing I could do was continue visualizing the jump done correctly, and rely on the many times I had landed it well before.

I worked hard to try to stay focused and positive, but in the days before the team short program, I encountered some boot issues. The rink at Capital Indoor Stadium was so warm and the ice so soft that after a practice session, my boots felt like they were made out of Play-Doh. That was a really big problem, because I like an extremely stiff boot in order to pull off my jumps. I go through maybe six or seven boots a season because I really rely on that stiffness for my jumps. Over the years, I've developed a great relationship with my boot maker, Raj Misir, at Jackson Ultima. I first met Raj back in 2010, through Ted Wilson, in China, and ever since, Jackson has been providing me boots and supporting my unusual needs. Like Raf and Brandon, Raj was also in uncharted territory in developing the right boot for the amount of training and jumping I did. Together, we had to figure out the right timing of when to switch out old boots for new ones. Before I started training quads regularly, I changed boots maybe two times a season, but once the quads started, I needed a lot more support for my takeoffs and landings. I would attribute 30 percent of my confidence in competition to my skates and how well they are holding up. At first, throughout my junior and early senior career, I would duct-tape my boots to get some extra support. That wasn't a durable solution, though, and we eventually came up with a rhythm of breaking in new boots three to four weeks before a competition. Even that depended a lot on guesswork, since leather varies and some boots would hold up longer than others. Ultimately I settled on breaking in new boots two weeks before I competed. Raf also got involved and started taking apart and building up my boots. In addition to his decades of jumping experience, Raf was also a master boot cobbler. I don't know how it started, but over the years he's become very good at mounting blades on boots and fixing any problems. Throughout my career, Raf had mounted my boots and was the first person I consulted with any issues I had. He even sent me to Yale with a bunch of tools and some basic tips for mounting my boots myself.

After a few sessions in Beijing, my two-week-old boots were already getting soft. I had dealt with soft boots before, but I was afraid these would only continue to get softer. I had a pair of backup boots, but they ended up having their own issues and I couldn't wear them. I had also brought a third pair, but they, too, were already a little soft. By this time, it was two days before the short program in the team event. Starting to panic, I went to Raf.

"Raf, you have to help me," I told him. I explained that while the sides of the boots were holding up, the center, with the tongue, was starting to collapse. He looked at the boots and we called over the U.S. Figure Skating skate technician, Mike Cunningham.

"Mike, what kind of leather do you have and what tools do you have?" Raf asked him.

Raf's idea was to reinforce the tongues of my skates with a piece of leather to stiffen them so I would feel more support in my ankle, which is where I needed it the most—that's where I bend to get the lift I need to pull off the quad jumps. We went back and forth, deciding what size and where exactly we would place those pieces of leather. We feared placing them in the wrong spot would cause a different part of the boot to break down prematurely and cause other issues. Mike and Raf ended up gluing a palm-sized flat piece of leather to the middle of each tongue, which gave me that extra support. I still can't believe how quickly Raf was able to figure out that solution. Had it not been for Mike having that specific leather, and the specific tools, and Raf having the intuition to determine exactly how to cut the leather to fit the tongue, my boots would have been toast before the competition even began.

Still, being the worrier that I am, I kept asking Raf: "Are you sure this is going to hold? Are you sure this leather will hold?"

He kept saying, "This is leather. It will hold. Push them hard and they will be fine. Don't worry about holding back, they will be fine."

Sure enough, they lasted through the team short program, the individual short program, the individual free program, and all the way through the exhibition skate. Raf knows his stuff.

The night before the team short program, I lay awake in my room. All I could think about was how I had felt four years ago, especially the two weeks leading up to PyeongChang—how debilitated I'd felt, how little confidence I'd had, and how I hadn't felt ready for the Olympics or strong enough to make it through the competition.

And then my mind drifted to how I'd felt when I got off the ice after that first short program in the team event. How embarrassed I'd felt, how disappointed I was, and just how terrible the whole experience was.

But as the worries snuck in, I countered them by visualizing me doing all my elements perfectly. I was worried about the last jump in the program, the quad Lutz–triple toe combination, which I'd been struggling with. Instead of thinking about falling or popping open on the jump, I saw myself with my body upright preparing for the jump, pulling my left outside edge through, tapping my right skate into the ice at just the right moment, pulling my arms into my body, and turning one, two, three, four times before landing perfectly on my right leg and tapping into the next jump. And if I worried that 2018 would happen again, I reminded myself that that experience had already happened, I had learned from it, and I had a new opportunity to compete at the Games.

The next morning, I got up at 4 A.M. because I had a 6:30 A.M. practice before I competed in the team event at 9:55 A.M. I'm not a morning person. At home I like to go to bed around 10 P.M., then get up in the morning and head to practice around 9 A.M. That night in Beijing, in order to get my ten hours of sleep, I got into bed at 5 P.M., and hoped to fall asleep by 6 P.M.

When I woke up, I started packing everything I needed for the competition. I knew I wouldn't have time to come back to the Village after practice since the arena was a thirty- to forty-minute bus ride away. I packed my skates, costume, socks, gel pads, skate guards, pomade to keep my hair in control during the competition, a few freeze-dried meals (I was finding them very useful!), some oatmeal, and chocolate milk, and headed to get tested. We had to get tested every day while we were in the Village, so I went upstairs to get my throat swabbed, but the center didn't open until 6. So I quickly ran over to the bus to catch the next shuttle to the rink and decided to get tested after the competition.

I got to the arena while the previous group of skaters was still practicing, so I watched them for a little while and then visualized my jumps on the ice.

After practice, Brandon and I headed to a special place where I could warm up for the competition and spend the rest of the morning before I skated. At Nationals, he had found me a little room that wasn't part of the main locker room that was quiet and isolated, which I loved. Given my worries about COVID-19, and also because I generally prefer being by myself before I compete, I really liked having a separate space where I could retreat before and after competing. Before coming to Beijing, I asked Brandon and Mitch if I could have a small room at Capital Indoor Stadium.

Brandon came through and found one next to the medical room that was near the entrance to the ice. It was put aside for the short track speed skaters, who were competing in the same arena on days that we were not. It was perfect. There was a physical therapy table where I could take a quick nap before I competed, had benches where I could sit and tie my skates, and it was warm.

After Brandon and I went through our stability and warm-up routine, I listened to my program music and visualized checking off each of my jumps and spins and moving through all my choreography.

Since 2018, I had made another big change in my competition routine—streamlining my warm-up routine. Out of necessity, because of the limited time I had to warm up before getting on the ice while I was at Yale, I had gradually whittled my routine from about an hour down to about thirty to forty minutes.

At competitions, I have so much adrenaline pumping that I could reasonably get ready to compete in only fifteen minutes. That season, I still got to the rink about an hour before my warm-up time, but I wouldn't start moving until about thirty to forty-five minutes before I had to get on the ice. Instead of doing a lengthy program of exercises, I also found that the best way to get my heart going and my body warmed up was to either dribble a basketball or toss a football around. I started playing basketball in 2016, after Tony took me to my first NBA game: the Utah Jazz playing the LA Clippers at the Staples Center. I was hooked. I had never seen basketball live, and it was so cool—the team chemistry, the physicality of the game, how fast-paced and precise the players are. I also thought it was fascinating to see how they dealt with the pressure of playing at such a high level.

So I started playing a bit. I was living in Long Beach at the time, before the 2018 Games, and there was a court about a four-minute bike ride from my apartment. Whenever I felt stressed out about skating, or needed to clear my head, I would bike to the court and shoot some hoops.

After the 2018 Olympics, while I was on tour, we stopped by an outlet mall with a Nike store. They were selling this baby basketball that I thought would be perfect to take on tour, and that's how I started dribbling and throwing the ball around as a way to warm up before skating because it got my heart pumping without tiring me out too much.

Then the Christmas before the 2022 Games, Janice gave me a football. In the month before the Olympics, I was spending my breaks outside to avoid close contact with anyone inside the rink. At Great Park there is a big grassy area in the front where no one really hangs out, so in between practice sessions I would eat lunch and relax there. I ended up tossing the ball there quite a few times—with my mom. I kept that habit up in Beijing, where Brandon Siakel and Michal Březina helped me out with that.

In Beijing, I made a habit of calling my mom before each of my events, between my warm-up and my time to compete. I would hydrate a freeze-dried meal and take it outside to eat, to stay safe from COVID-19. It was so cold that my phone battery would drain, but I always brought a spare battery. We would talk for about twenty minutes about my training and my recovery. She was in San Francisco at Janice's house, so I would sometimes chat with Janice, Orestes, my dad, and Colin as well, once they got there.

Still, by the time my name was called, right before I stepped onto the ice for the team event, while I was physically prepared, mentally, I felt similar to the way I had in 2018 before the team event: weak, unstable, and not at all ready. Before I have some of my best skates,

I generally feel amped-up, like when you're in the gym and trying to set a personal record on a rep or something. At the competitions in which I skate my worst, I feel like my body and mind are not connected and I'm trying to do something that my body is physically unable to do. I had that feeling in 2018 and it was sneaking back in at Beijing.

But there was a difference. In 2018 I tried to change the outcome and force myself to feel amped, which didn't work. This time, I knew I couldn't change the way that I felt, but needed to redirect my mind to think about all the perfect jumps and clean programs I had done. Even if my body didn't feel prepared, I had done this program multiple times cleanly back-to-back, so I reminded myself that I could definitely do it now with fresh legs. I also reminded myself that, yes, I could make mistakes, but my body knew how to launch myself into the air, spin four times, and land cleanly on the correct edge to execute a perfect jump. Eric always emphasized that how I felt wasn't as important as how I told myself to feel.

I kept all this in mind as I skated to center ice to take my starting position. As soon as I hit my pose, I knew that this time around, I could rely on my training and experience over the past four years.

Just as there were in 2018, for the team event, there were boxes rink side for the teams from each of the ten countries competing, where your teammates sat to cheer you on. Seeing the Team USA box in 2018 I thought, "Man, this is stressful." All I could feel were the eyes of my fellow skaters on me and the pressure to perform because how I did affected how many points my team received. But relying on the new mental skills I had learned, I flipped that pressure around into gratitude and used the presence of my teammates to pull me through the program.

I landed all three of my jumps. Each time I landed one, I could hear my teammates yell and it gave me a lot of confidence to know they were all there supporting me. Hitting my final pose, I felt a wave of relief. Afterward, the media predictably put out stories about redemption and getting the monkey of 2018 off my back. But I didn't necessarily see it that way. As soon as I left the ice, I immediately starting thinking about how I could top that in a few days when I had to compete the same program for the men's individual short program. I was happy, yes, but didn't let myself celebrate too much.

The team short program was a good trial run for the jump layout I was planning for the individual competition a few days later. At Nationals, I had done the quad flip for my first jump, and the more technically challenging quad Lutz–triple toe combination in the second half of the program for the first time. For Beijing, I wanted to maximize my points, so decided to repeat that layout, putting the quad Lutz and triple toe combination in the second half—which would give me that extra 10 percent bonus—and keep the quad flip as the first jump. I know that in their NBC commentary, Tara and Johnny made a lot of this decision and guessed that the main reason I made it was to collect more points.

That was true, but I had other reasons as well.

I tend to land the quad Lutz more reliably if I put it in combination with another jump. Knowing that I need momentum after the Lutz to pop back up into a second jump helps me pull more flow out of the Lutz than if the Lutz is a solo jump. The Lutz also takes a lot more control to pull off. I go into the jump with my skate blade curving in one direction, but once I jump into the air, I have to rotate my body in the opposite direction. My technique is largely dependent on how much I can cut into the ice and how deep an edge I can get for that jump, which depends on how mobile my ankle is.

After the six-minute warm-up, I get off the ice while the other skaters compete and take my boots off before I have to skate again. With all my nervous energy, I tend to retie my skates extraordinarily tightly, which makes it hard for me to bend at my ankle. If I can't get a deep enough edge on the Lutz take-off, I can't vault myself into the air high enough to get all four revolutions in. Having the Lutz in the second half of my program when my ankles are more warmed up and my boots are more flexible made sense—even though I would be more tired by then. However, if I can pull my edge through just right, I use much less energy than on the quad flip, so putting it in the second half of the program made sense to me. It was a calculated risk, but I felt more comfortable with the quad Lutz–triple toe combination in the second half. Plus, doing the flip first would set me up well for the rest of the program, because I can land it pretty well when I have energy, and if I hit that first jump, I feed off the momentum and maintain that pace.

It worked well in the team short program, so my plan was to do the same for the men's individual short program, which was four days later. But now that I had skated well, the pressure was on. I had to skate at least as well as I had in the team event, if not better.

After the team event concluded, Team USA placed second and we were supposed to have our team medal ceremony the night before the men's short program. The timing was challenging for the men, since we had to compete the following morning, and we probably wouldn't be able to get a full night's rest after the late-night ceremony. I asked the USOPC officials if I could skip the medal ceremony because I had to compete the next morning. I didn't want to miss the chance to celebrate with my teammates, but I really needed the full night's rest before my individual event. Mitch spoke to the other teams that had earned medals, Russia and Japan, and they all agreed that the medal ceremony timing wasn't ideal for the skaters in the men's event. The three teams that earned medals wrote a joint letter asking if the medal ceremony could be postponed until after the individual men's short program, since we would have the next day off to rest before the free program competition the following day. The Olympic organizers agreed and we planned to have the medal ceremony right after the men's short.

So now, my focus was all on the question—how would I pull off another clean short program? Over the next few days, this made me very nervous. Even at the end of my short program in the team event, while I was skating the footwork sequence, I remember thinking, "Man, I wish this were the individual short program because this is pretty solid." If I could perform the way I had there in the individual competition, I would have been pretty happy. Now all I could think was, "I have to do it again." I talked to Eric about how to get past that concern. Even though I had skated well in the team competition, if I screwed up the short program in the men's event, I would be in the exact same situation that I had found myself during the 2018 Games. He continued to remind me that instead of focusing on what could go wrong, I should concentrate on the many, many times things had gone well, when I had executed the program cleanly. He urged me to continue visualizing perfectly executed programs. And he continued to ask me to emphasize visualizing the jumps that I was worried about, and picture myself landing them.

For my short program, I skated in the last group of six athletes, following several of my main competitors—Yuzuru Hanyu, Shoma Uno, and Yuma Kagiyama. As each of them skated, I kept a close eye on which elements they did and how they skated. It's a quirk I have of needing to know what's going on in real time during my competitions. Some skaters refuse to know and find it nerve-racking, but for me, I get more anxious if I don't know how the other skaters performed.

Knowing that some of them hadn't skated perfectly, I immediately started to calculate whether I should stick with the more challenging quad Lutz–triple toe in the second half of my program, or whether I could sub in the easier quad toe–triple toe. But I hadn't trained that jump most of the season, while I had worked on the quad Lutz–triple toe combination. That was my mom's argument in 2018—that I should stick with the program that I had trained, and the program that my body knew, rather than switching things around.

Having learned my lesson, I decided to stick with the quad Lutz–triple toe, but even so, during the program, I still had a split second of hesitation during my spin—the flip and Axel had gone well, so I thought maybe I should just do the quad toe–triple toe and play it safe. But I corrected myself. I pushed away any doubts, focused on the jump, and thought, "Stop, that's like telling yourself that you're weak, and that you're not capable of doing this. You are strong, just do it."

I went for the quad Lutz–triple toe and landed it.

I don't know if anyone watching could tell, but after that last jump, inside I was screaming, "Yes! Yes! Yes!" I was so thrilled. I was so relieved to get through that jump combination, and to get through a second clean short program at the Olympics. Finally. But I was similarly happy at Nationals during the free program and then tripped during the footwork sequence. The footwork and final spin in the short program are important point grabbers, too, so I knew I wasn't quite done yet. I told myself: stay in control, control your steps, divert your emotion into the program and into the character of the program instead.

When I finished that final spin, I couldn't help myself—I was so excited that I pumped my fist into the air.

Yes!

Tara and Johnny, who were commentating on the Games, were surprised—and happy—by that and said, correctly, that I rarely show emotion after I skate. If I'm too out there with my emotions after I compete, I feel like I'm not being respectful. But at that moment? I couldn't help it. I was so happy to get over that hurdle. That "monkey" had been on my back for so long, and to finally throw it off and have two solid short program skates at the Olympics that I could be happy and proud of was huge.

It was even sweeter because I set a personal best and a world record with that performance. I don't usually dwell much on my scores from different events because I don't think you can really compare scores from one competition to another—the judging panels are different, so points aren't always comparable between National Championships to World Championships and even Grand Prix events. At face value, the scores don't necessarily explain everything.

That said, scores are the most quantitative way of keeping track of how you're doing and of how you are improving. When I saw my score from the team short program, I was really excited to see it continue to inch upward. After the team event, I felt I had done pretty much everything I could to get my highest score possible, so I wasn't entirely sure how I could improve on that in the men's individual short program. I decided I would try to make everything a little cleaner, starting with landing the jumps more precisely, making every edge in the footwork crisper, and making my spins a little faster so I could earn as many additional points as I could.

It worked. I ended up eking out more than two more points in my technical score to set that personal best and world record.

I was ready to face my next challenge, the free program. But before that, the Olympics were hit with some surprising news. Just as our team finished getting dressed and ready to go to the team medal ceremony, we were told that it was being postponed indefinitely due to a legal matter. None of us knew at the time that a skater had tested positive for a banned substance, so the standings, and the medal ceremony, had to be postponed until the situation had been investigated and resolved. Since we had no idea what was going on and all of us had more competitions coming up, we left and got ready for bed.

Going into the free program two days later, I had a nearly six-point lead, and that was reassuring. Given that margin, I talked to my mom about whether it made sense to scale down my jumps in the free program. Not surprisingly, she disagreed, the same way she had been against filling my mind with two different short programs in 2018. She had the same argument that she had had back then: I had trained the program with the harder jumps and had had success with them, so why switch when my body wouldn't be used to a different jump layout? Raf also agreed with her, mainly because he said he knew I had proven all season that I could execute the harder program.

That ultimately made the difference for me. In 2018, my mind was reeling from training those two programs, which meant neither layout was consistent in training. In Beijing, I knew that the right approach was to stick to my planned program content. Throughout my practices in Beijing, I had been training the harder program and was confident I could pull it off.

For the free program competition, you skate in reverse finishing order from the short program, so I skated last, my least favorite starting position. I hate waiting after I get off the ice after the six-minute warm-up, and I hate the nerves of anticipating how the other skaters do. That's partly why I track the competition while it's unfolding, because that way I don't have to worry or get anxious about what might happen—I can just look at the screens and know. I tracked the last group of six, until Yuma, who skated just before me.

I was sort of "watching" the live event on my phone, checking Jackie Wong's live Twitter feed of results as Shoma skated, because I was in a semisecluded hallway where there weren't any screens. And I was gauging how well he skated by listening to the reaction of the people in the audience. He had a good score, so I knew I had to pull off all my elements cleanly.

Since I skated right after Yuma, I was in the arena while he competed, in that tiny, terrifying curtained-off area by the rink. The area is not closed on top, so when I looked up I could see Yuma on the jumbo screen over the rink. I watched him land his quad Salchow and knew the score was going to be high. Yuma stepped out of his quad loop and wasn't able to do the second part of his first jump combination, but then threw in a three-jump combo in the second half of his program, including a quad toe. This was going to be a challenge.

I redirected my energy back to my mindset. Being in that space was still terrifying, but I reminded myself that I wanted to be there, that I was grateful to be there, that I was going to have fun, and that I had worked hard to compete at another Olympics.

While Yuma was waiting for his scores, I got on the ice for my two minutes of warm-up. I have a system for going through my jumps in this short period of time, so I worked through my routine, starting with my triples—triple Axel, triple flip, triple Lutz, and then the triple Salchow—the one I was most worried about doing as a quad in my program. There is no other way to put it—those triple Salchows in that warm-up were awful, awful, awful. I just couldn't get the takeoff that I wanted; every time I pushed into the inside edge, my foot collapsed inward and I lost height on the takeoff. Those were the worst triple Salchows I did the entire time I was in Beijing.

I started to feel anxious but made a conscious effort to turn that frustration around, as Eric and I had talked about. I knew why I couldn't get the lift I needed, so I just focused on fixing the error, which I had done a million times. I knew I needed to be patient and think about shooting my body backward to get the revolutions I needed, even if my takeoff wasn't ideal.

In the program, while my takeoff was rocky, by focusing all my energy on sending my body backward, I managed to turn one, two, three, four times and then land without falling. It was a little shaky, but I stood up, so I knew I had done the right thing. It was definitely not one of my best-landed quad Salchow jumps, but I was honestly more proud of it than more cleanly landed ones. In the past, given how badly the warm-up had gone, I would have popped or fallen on that jump. But I salvaged it because I knew that I would probably have a weak takeoff—and I knew how to adjust for it.

After hitting my quad Lutz, I was thrilled because my most difficult jumps were out of the way, and I knew I just had to stay on my feet. One of my last jumping passes is a three-jump combination, the quad toe–Euler–triple flip; I landed the quad but didn't have enough momentum to pull back into a triple flip so I ended up singling that. I knew I had the option of swapping the triple flip for a triple Salchow, but I had tried that in practice and it pushed me off my pattern in the program and led me to miss my triple Axel. So I knew my best bet was to let that jump combination go, and conserve my energy for a nice triple Axel. After that, I had one more triple Lutz–triple toe combo and my big hitters were done, so I told myself to just enjoy the footwork sequence that closed the program and not to get too excited and fall again like I had at Nationals. To make that footwork really stand out, I needed to bring my energy level back up to match the excitment and pace of the music at that point. I still had a minor slip on my slide because I was leaning a little too far back; but, man, when it was done, that footwork was so much fun. I couldn't help but grin ear to ear, thinking, "I think I just did it. I think I just won the Olympics." For a moment, I did think, "Ma is going to be upset about that toe flip." But once I sat down in the kiss and cry and saw my score, I let myself get over that. I was glad I had decided to stick with the higher technical content, since I needed all the points I could get.

I had done it. After a terrible first Olympic experience in 2018, I trusted myself to train for another four years for a chance to experience a better one. And after all the hours at the rink, after all the doubts—after all that, I saw the number 1 next to my name, which meant I was the Olympic champion. I was taking home a gold medal.

After my scores came up, the first thing Raf said to me was, "We made it!" At first, I obviously thought he meant winning gold, but, funnily enough, he was actually joking about not getting COVID-19.

I was truly happy for Raf, too. After everything we had been through, I owed him a lot for making me the skater that I am. Throughout the season, he kept telling me, "Nathan, I've never coached a skater who won an Olympic title before, and I don't know if I am going to have another opportunity to bring another skater to the Olympics and put them in a position where they might win. Nathan, you are my last hope."

When he would tell me this, my first thought would be "What if I can't make it happen?"

That entire season, I told myself I wasn't training for Raf or for my mom or for anyone else but myself. But after winning Olympic gold, I allowed myself to realize that it wasn't just for myself; I wasn't alone in the journey.

At the medal ceremony, I lifted the medal and felt its weight—it was much heavier than I expected it to be. It was finally mine. Once it was around my neck, I thought of my mom, who I knew was watching back in California and had sacrificed so much so that I could skate and turn my childhood dream of being an Olympic champion into reality. I could see Brandon Siakel, who got pretty emotional watching me because he had been there through all those years of ups and downs and injuries and recovery, and those many hours in the gym. I also saw Mitch Moyer, who had provided so many of the opportunities and guidance I needed to accomplish this goal. My medical team, without whose help I would not have been able to make it through my career. And of course Raf, who was in the crowd dancing and being ridiculous because he was so happy. We had done it. Together.

Yes!

EPILOGUE

My performances in Beijing will always be a highlight of my life and represent to me so much more than a single medal can convey. The only thing that took away from the experience from winning gold was not having my family there in Beijing to celebrate with me. Throughout my life, my parents and siblings have been my foundation and sacrificed so much to make it possible for me to skate and pursue my Olympic dream—not just once but twice.

After my press conference while I was waiting for the required drug testing, I was finally able to really talk to them. My parents, Janice, Orestes, and Colin were together in San Francisco at Janice and Orestes's place. Alice had just moved to New York, so she watched with her boyfriend from there. Tony and his girlfriend were in Portugal, so they stayed up all night to watch. Yuki joined by Zoom from New York. They were all so happy for me, and it felt really good to hear that.

It's funny, because my first thought after I finished was about what my mom would say about my missed jump combination. True to form, seconds into the call, she asked me, "What happened with the quad toe–triple flip? Why did you make that mistake?" That was exactly her. I explained I hadn't gotten enough momentum out of the toe to finish the triple flip. I know she wasn't blaming me, or trying to be overly critical, but pointing it out to make sure I understood what went wrong and hopefully not repeat the same mistake. That's been the way she has grounded me throughout my entire skating career, reminding me that every mistake was a learning opportunity to make the fewest possible mistakes in the future. It's kept me, and all my siblings, humble and pushing forward.

Later, my mom told me that when she watched the medal ceremony and saw me put the gold medal around my neck, the thoughts about my mistake vanished. Instead, she was filled with emotion and thought only about the twenty years of hard work we had put in and all the people who had helped me on my journey. She said she was proud of me for finally achieving my goal.

I felt the same way.

I realized that with all the excitement in Beijing after the competition, I had never properly thanked my mom for everything she had done to make my gold possible. After getting back to the United States, I went on the *Today* show in New York to talk about my experience at the Olympics. To my surprise, NBC had secretly flown my mom in to join me. In the middle of the interview, my mom walked on set. It was the first time I had seen her in over a month, and since winning gold. I was so shocked, and in such a rush to give her my medal, that I didn't even give her time to sit down before hanging it around her neck. She and I have been through so much together that I didn't feel I needed to explain—giving her my medal and saying thank you in person was enough.

Winning gold as the first Asian American and Chinese American man in men's figure skating wouldn't have been possible without all of the Asian American skaters that came before me. I hope my medal can make another Asian American kid feel he or she too can achieve their dreams through hard work and perseverance. I don't know where my skating career will take me next, but I know that I will be forever grateful for everything that it has brought me. Skating has enriched my life so much that I will somehow always find my way back to the ice rink. My next goal is to go back to Yale and make the most of my last two years there. Leading up to the Games, I wasn't able to fully take advantage of all that being a college student has to offer, and I hope I can now that I have the time. I've decided to pursue a degree in statistics and data science, but haven't decided what I'll do after that. I'm pretty sure I want to continue my education with postgraduate work, whether that will be in statistics or medical school.

During my first two years at Yale, I was surrounded by classmates who have done amazing things and had incredible experiences and impressive ideas to make the world a better place. I hope to dedicate myself to doing more for others. I'm not exactly sure how, but I want to spend my remaining two years in college trying to figure that out.

During my time in this sport, I've been so fortunate to skate alongside an incredible generation of skaters who pushed the sport forward in so many different ways. Being part of the evolution in men's figure skating, where athletes are executing these insanely difficult programs that have never been done before, means a lot to me. I never would have been able to reach my goals without the competitive push of those athletes. Pushing the limits of what I could do was something that drove me forward as an athlete. I'm so excited to see where the sport moves next, and can't wait for what's to come.

Skating has brought me to my highest highs, as well as my lowest lows. There were times when I achieved goals that I never believed were possible. There were also times after bad practices I wanted to throw my skates against the locker doors, and thought about never putting those skates on again. But each time, I knew in my heart that skating has, and always will be, a part of me. Standing on the Olympic podium with my gold medal wasn't the end of my journey. I'll approach whatever comes next—in skating or in life—the same way I always have, from those first steps on the ice in Salt Lake City to my final program in Beijing: one jump at a time.

ACKNOWLEDGMENTS

I have realized that accomplishing my Olympic dream has been the result of a team of people that have supported me, pushed me, and stood beside me the entire way. This Olympic journey is as much theirs as it is mine. My deepest gratitude to all that helped me get there.

I want to thank my agent, Yuki Saegusa, for bringing me the opportunity to tell the story of my skating life. Yuki has been my biggest champion since she spoke to me and my mom at a skating competition in 2016, when she saw something in me that none of us did at the time. She has become like a member of our family, and I can't thank her enough for all the opportunities she has provided for me, and for supporting me through the ups and downs.

I also have to thank Sheryl Shade, an agent and manager of numerous Olympic athletes, who thought that my story would be worth telling in a book. And I'm grateful to Lisa Sharkey at HarperCollins for agreeing and being an enthusiastic advocate of the book from the start. Their encouragement helped me to really enjoy the process of sharing my story.

My biggest thank you must go to Alice Park, my writer, who has helped put into words all my reflections from my career on the ice. From our initial discussion of the framework of the book, to the countless hours we spent on the phone tracing my journey, to our back-and-forth exchanges on the many revisions of the book, Alice has always been understanding, patient, and paid great attention to detail. It's been an honor to be able to be a part of this project with her.

I'm deeply grateful for Maddie Pillari at HarperCollins who improved the draft with her edits, and the rest of the team at Harper-Collins that created the sharply designed final product. Thank you to Bonni Leon-Berman for the look of the chapter openers and interior of the book and Jared Oriel for designing the cover. I also want to thank editorial assistant Emilia Marroquin, Kate D'Esmond and Tina Andreadis in publicity, and Leah Wasielewski and Becca Putnam in marketing for helping my book reach more people. And a special thanks to Jonathan Burnham for supporting the idea of a figure skating book. I'd also like to thank Professor Michael Berry 白睿文, Director of the Center for Chinese Studies at UCLA, for his translation of the Chinese proverbs included in the book.

A special thank you to Henry and Susan Samueli and Vicky Chun for providing me the ice time I needed to work for my dreams. Throughout my skating career, so many people have generously shared their time, expertise, and support to keep me on the ice—I would not be the skater I am today without the help of all of them, from each of my coaches and choreographers, doctors and physical therapists, to my boot and blade makers and the technicians who sharpened my blades. Not all of them get the attention they deserve, and I especially want to thank the team that has kept my boots in perfect shape and blades consistent and razor sharp through the years, giving me the confidence I need to improve my skating. Karel Kovar, Stewart Sturgeon, Mike Cummingham, Raj Misir, Kevin Wu, Tom Cantwell, Dennie Jacques, Bruce Surdin, John Register, Serhii Vaypan, and Michal Brezina— thank you for always being ready, almost always at short notice, to give my skates the edge I needed.

I was also very fortunate to have great teachers in the ELP program, who made sure I got an excellent education despite my spending so much time at the rink. I am forever grateful to Carolyn Zaugg, Mindy Byrnes, Dawn Savage, Leslie Edwards, Marilyn Taft, Julie Anzelmo, and Julie Lloyd Henderson for their academic guidance. I would also like to thank the city of Salt Lake—for being my home, and for hosting the 2002 Olympics. Those Games gave me the inspiration and opportunity to become an athlete, and an Olympian. Having so many wonderful rinks on which to skate introduced me to the sport of figure skating, and I am grateful for that. My career wouldn't be possible without the support of Salt Lake Figure Skating. Thank you for creating the environment for me to grow.

Finally, thank you to my family for supporting me when I decided to write this book. This is our family's story, and I couldn't tell it without you. Without you, I might not have stepped on the ice, and without your constant encouragement, I definitely would not have continued getting up every time I fell.

PHOTO CREDITS

ABOUT THE AUTHOR

On February 10, 2022, Nathan Chen redefined men's figure skating, winning the Olympic gold medal and cementing his position as "Quad King," a name bestowed upon him after the 2017 U.S. Figure Skating Championships when Chen became the first man in figure skating history to land five quadruple jumps in a single performance. Born in Salt Lake City, home of the 2002 Olympic Winter Games, Chen began skating at age three, as Olympic spirit fueled the city. After an Olympic debut in 2018 that earned him fifth place, Chen went on to win three World Championships, six Grand Prix events, two Grand Prix Finals, and a total of six U.S. titles. Chen was also named the 2019 Team USA Male Olympic Athlete of the Year and was included in 2019 Forbes' 30 Under 30 list. When Chen returned to the Olympics in 2022, he performed a soaring free skate set to Elton John's *Rocketman* and secured an Olympic title, which established him as the first Asian American male skater to do so. When asked who he dedicates his gold medal to, Chen said, "My mother. No one deserves it more, and I am forever grateful for her never-ending support."